POETRY AND POETS

POETRY AND POETS

Essays

BY
AMY LOWELL

BIBLO and TANNEN
NEW YORK
1971

Reprinted, 1971, by permission

by

Biblo & Tannen Booksellers and Publishers, Inc.
63 Fourth Avenue   New York, N.Y. 10003

Library of Congress Catalog Card Number. 77-162298

SBN-8196-0274-4

114098

Printed in U.S.A. by
NOBLE OFFSET PRINTERS, INC.
NEW YORK 3, N. Y.

PREFACE

So great was the energy and industry of Amy Lowell in the long nights that made her working days that during her lifetime publication never kept pace with production. At her untimely death, following soon after the appearance of her monumental 'John Keats,' three volumes of poems were practically ready for the press. These three — 'Ballads for Sale,' 'East Wind,' and 'What's O'Clock,' — together with a volume of 'Selected Poems,' have now been published.

Besides the poems, her portfolios contained a large amount of prose — manuscripts, magazine articles, interviews, miscellanea — some of it purely ephemeral and 'timely' in interest, but much of it that characteristic, eager prose, known to readers of her 'Tendencies' and 'Six French Poets,' setting forth robustly her considered opinions on many matters of permanent literary interest. From this material there has been selected for publication three groups of essays or articles dealing with poetry and poets. These are presented in the following pages: four essays on what poetry is and how it is made; two on elder poets in whose work Miss Lowell found special meaning for herself; and seven short essays on the work of her leading poetic contemporaries. In all of them her familiar voice speaks with resonance and authority.

CONTENTS

ON POETRY

ON ELDER POETS

CONTEMPORARIES

ON POETRY

WHY WE SHOULD READ POETRY

WHY should one read Poetry? That seems to me a good deal like asking: Why should one eat? One eats because one has to, to support life, but every time one sits down to dinner one does not say, 'I must eat this meal so that I may not die.' On the contrary, we eat because we are hungry, and so eating appears to us as a pleasant and desirable thing to do.

The necessity for poetry is one of the most fundamental traits of the human race. But naturally we do not take that into account, any more than we take into account that dinner, and the next day again, dinner, is the condition of our remaining alive. Without poetry the soul and heart of man starves and dies. The only difference between them is that all men know, if they turn their minds to it, that without food they would die, and comparatively few people know that without poetry they would die.

When trying to explain anything, I usually find that the Bible, that great collection of magnificent and varied poetry, has said it before in the best possible way. Now the Bible says that 'man shall not live by bread alone.' Which, in modern words, means — cannot live on the purely material things. It is true, he cannot, and he never does. If he did, every bookshop would shut, every theatre would close its doors, every florist and picture dealer would go out of business, even the baseball grounds would close. For what is baseball but a superb epic of man's swiftness and sureness, and his putting forth the utmost of the sobriety and vigour that is in him in an ecstasy of vitality and movement? And the men who watch are carried away by this ecstasy, out of themselves and the routine of their daily lives, into a world romantic with physical force. But you object that they don't think of it in this way. Of course they don't; if they did they would be poets, and most men are not poets. But this is really what stirs them, for without it, throwing a little ball about a field, and trying to hit it with a stick, isn't really very interesting. A baseball game is a sort of moving picture of what Homer wrote in his Iliad. I do not believe there is a boy in America who would not like Butcher and Lang's translation of the Odyssey, if no one had ever told him it was a schoolbook.

That is what poetry really is. It is the height and quintessence of emotion, of every sort of emotion. But it is always somebody feeling something at white heat, and it is as vital as the description of a battle would be, told by a soldier who had been in it.

I do not wish to be misunderstood. I do not mean that every book, or every play, contains this true poetry. Many, most, alas! are poor imitations; some are merely sordid and vulgar. But books and plays exist because man is groping for a life beyond himself, for a beauty he needs, and is seeking to find. And the books and plays which live are those which satisfy this need.

Somebody once said to me that to make goodness dull was a great crime. In poetry, those men who have written without original and vital feeling, without a flaming imagination, have much to answer for. It is owing to them that poetry has come to mean a stupid and insipid sort of stuff, quite remote from people's lives, fit only for sentimental youth and nodding old age. That sort of poetry is what is technically called 'derivative,' which means that the author copies some one else's emotion, often some one else's words, and commonplace verses are written about flowers, and moonlight, and love, and death, by people who would never be moved by any of these things if sincere poets had not been writing about them from the beginning of the world. People who like to hear the things they are used to repeated say, 'That is beautiful poetry'; simple, straightforward people say, 'Perhaps it is. But I don't care for poetry.' But once in a while there comes along a man with knowledge and courage enough to say, 'That is not poetry at all, but insincere bosh!'

Again I do not mean that all poetry can be enjoyed by everybody. People have different tastes and different training. A man at forty seldom cares for the books which delighted him as a boy. People stop developing at all ages. Some men never mature beyond their teens; others go on growing and changing until old age. Because B likes a book is no reason why A should. And we are the inheritors of so splendid a literature that there are plenty of books for everybody. Many people enjoy Kipling's poems who would be confused by Keats; others delight in Burns who would be utterly without sympathy for Blake. The people who like Tennyson do not, as a rule, care much about Walt Whitman, and the admirers of Poe and Coleridge may find Wordsworth unattractive, and again his disciples might feel antagonized by Rossetti and Swinburne. It does not matter, so long as one finds one's own sustenance. Only, the happy men who can enjoy them all are the richest. The true test of poetry is sincerity and vitality. It is not rhyme, or metre, or subject. It is nothing in the world but the soul of man as it really is. Carlyle's 'French Revolution' is a great epic poem; so are Trevelyan's three volumes on 'Garibaldi and the Italian War of Independence.' That they are written in prose has nothing to do with the matter. That most poems are written rhythmically, and that rhythm has come to be the great technical fact of poetry, was, primarily, because men under stress of emotion tend to talk in a rhythmed speech. Read Lincoln's 'Address at Gettysburg' and 'Second Inaugural,' and you will see.

Nothing is more foolish than to say that only such and such forms are proper to poetry. Every form is proper to poetry, so long as it is the sincere expression of a man's thought. That insincere men try bizarre forms of verse to gain a personal notoriety is true, but it seems not very difficult to distinguish them from the real artists. And so long as men feel, and think, and have the need of expressing themselves, so long will their modes of expression change. For expression tends to become hackneyed and devitalized, and new methods must be found for keeping the sense of palpitant vigour.

There are signs that we are living at the beginning of a great poetic renaissance. Only three weeks ago the 'New York Times' printed some remarks of Mr. Brett, the head of The Macmillan Company, in which he said that poetry was pushing itself into the best-seller class. And the other day a London publisher, Mr. Heinemann, announced that he should not publish so many novels, as they were a drug on the market. England has several magazines devoted exclusively to poetry and poetic drama. Masefield is paid enormous sums for his work, and a little book entitled 'The Georgian Book of Poetry,' containing the work of some of the younger men, which has been out barely two years, is already in its ninth edition. Here, in America, we have 'The Poetry Journal,' published in Boston, and 'Poetry,' published in Chicago. England counts among her poets W. B. Yeats, Robert Bridges, John Masefield, Wilfred Wilson Gibson, D. H. Lawrence, F. L. Flint, James Stevens, Rudyard Kipling, and, although on a somewhat more popular level, Alfred Noyes. England also boasts, as partly her own, the Bengal poet, Rabindranath Tagore, who has just been awarded the Nobel Prize, and Ezra Pound, who, although an American by birth and happily therefore ours to claim, lives in London. In America we have Josephine Preston Peabody, Bliss Carman, Edwin Arlington Robinson, Anna Hempstead Branch, Hermann Hagedorn, Grace Fallow Norton, Fanny Stearns Davis, and Nicholas Vachel Lindsay. These lists represent poets with many differing thoughts and modes of thought, but they point to the great vitality of poetry at the moment.

Have I answered the question? I think I have. We should read poetry because only in that way can we know man in all his moods — in the most beautiful thoughts of his heart, in his farthest reaches of imagination, in the tenderness of his love, in the nakedness and awe of his soul confronted with the terror and wonder of the Universe.

Poetry and history are the textbooks to the heart of man, and poetry is at once the most intimate and the most enduring.

POETRY AS A SPOKEN ART

To speak of poetry as a 'spoken art,' may seem, in this age of printing, a misnomer; and it is just because of such a point of view that the essential kinship of poetry and music is so often lost sight of. The 'beat' of poetry, its musical quality, is exactly that which differentiates it from prose, and it is this musical quality which bears in it the stress of emotion without which no true poetry can exist. Prose itself when it is fused with emotion becomes rhythmic, and the rhythm in turn heightens the emotional effect. The great orators of all time have been great because of their power to achieve this effect. Poetry and oratorical prose have this in common, that they are both intended primarily to be heard, not seen.

We moderns read so much more than we listen, that perhaps it is no wonder if we get into the habit of using our minds more than our ears, where literature is concerned, with the result that our imaginative, mental ear becomes absolutely atrophied. What I mean by our imaginative, mental ear is this: Most of us possess quite a handsome degree of visual imagination. In reading a book, we visualize its scenes. If we are reading about an orchard with an old stone seat set in an angle under blossoming boughs, we see the orchard, and the seat, with a good deal of distinctness, before us. Of course, the degree to which we see it depends upon how highly developed our imaginative power is. But I have never met any one so devoid of all such power as not to visualize to some extent the scenes of the story he was reading.

Now here is a curious thing: In the case of the average person, auditory imagination is not nearly so well developed as visual. Why this should be, I do not know. Possibly it is the writer's fault, or rather misfortune; it may be easier to convey the impression of a sight than of a sound. Whatever the cause may be that we do not hear things off paper as well as we see them, the fact, I believe, is indisputable.

No art has suffered so much from printing as has poetry. Our cheap processes of colour reproduction do not really reproduce the picture whose name they bear; they are merely so many shorthand notes upon it. If we have seen the picture, they serve to remind us of it; if we have not, they give us a kind of passport introduction to it when we meet it. They in no way attempt to replace the original picture; that exists apart from them, and no one would think of studying art by these reproductions alone. In the case of photographs, we have a still more restricted form of memoranda. For in photography, colours can only be given as light and shade. Photographs of paintings are more satisfactory than colour reproductions, because the imagination has more scope and does its work infinitely better than any mechanical colour process can do.

But take the case of poetry. Here we have no galleries of original pieces to which the art-hungry can turn. The reproduction, the printed book, is the only tangible substance which poetry has. If photography and colour-printing are the conventionalized symbols of pictures, how much slighter, less adequate, are the conventionalized symbols of poetry. Printed words, of no beauty in themselves, of no value except to rouse the imagination and cause it to function.

Again, take the case of music. Here we have a condition almost exactly similar to that of poetry, except for one thing. Printed notes are no more beautiful than printed words, but here comes in the one saving fact: nobody (except highly trained musicians) expects to *read* music, everybody insists upon *hearing* it.

Poetry is as much an art to be heard as is music, if we could only get people to understand the fact. To read it off the printed pages without pronouncing it is to get only a portion of its beauty, and yet it is just this that most people do.

Of course, the reason here is very simple. Wordsworth's 'Ode to Immortality' is manufactured with the very same tools we employ when we order the dinner. The tools in both cases are words. Everybody uses words, and uses them all the time. The most uneducated peasant talks. Words are the birthright of humanity. To be dumb is to be deformed.

Using the common implements of all the world, poetry is treated with a cavalier ease which music escapes. A long and special training is required to learn and understand music. The layman does not carry a musical score home in his pocket to read in the evening. If he wants to hear Debussy's 'L'Après-midi d'un Faune,' for instance, he goes to a concert, where an orchestra of carefully trained musicians interprets it for him.

Poetry will come into its Paradise when carefully trained speakers make a business of interpreting it to the world. And poetry needs such interpretation, for I suppose it is only one reader out of a hundred (and I think that percentage is rather high than otherwise) who can possibly get all the beauty out of a poem.

Every one knows that poetry existed before printing, and I imagine there is no doubt that it existed before writing, although, of course, that cannot be proved. Even so recently as the Middle Ages, troubadours went from castle to castle chanting their poems to delighted listeners. For people listened then, partly because they could not read, and also because, even if they could, there were so few books. With the rise of printing, with the advent of a reading populace, poetry ceased to be chanted, ceased to be read aloud at all for the most part; and the poet has suffered as a composer would suffer whose works were doomed to be rendered by no finer instrument than an accordion.

Shakespeare is the greatest English poet who has ever existed, and doubtless he would have been considered so under all circumstances. But Shakespeare has certainly enjoyed one inestimable advantage over all purely lyric poets — he has been acted for three hundred years, and that means that he has been spoken. People have heard his poetry rendered by men and women of extraordinary genius, who have spent their lives in studying it. The world has been forced to receive his poetry, the whole of his poetry, all its beauty of sound and content. There has been no excuse for misunderstanding him, and he has not been misunderstood. To hear a man like Forbes-Robertson speak Hamlet's words is like hearing

Kreisler play Bach, an experience never to be forgotten.

It is because we so seldom hear poetry adequately rendered that the art has for so long lapsed in popular favour. For years only those people trained to receive it as audible impression through the sense of sight have been able thoroughly to comprehend it. The few people who attempt to read it aloud are handicapped by the realization of the unusual quality of their task, and lose their sense of proportion and simplicity in the welter of artistic theories of expression which have gradually come into being. Let us examine a few of these theories, and see in what way they have hampered the enjoyment of poetry, and its simple, straightforward appeal.

I remember once hearing Sir Johnston Forbes-Robertson say that there was a good tradition of acting, and a poor tradition, and that because the latter existed was no reason to decry the former. That is as true of the reading of poetry aloud as of acting. But the trouble is that the good tradition is only one, and there are ninety and nine poor traditions to balance it. At least, actors have some training, but with poetry readers, if they have any, it is invariably one of the ninety and nine. I suppose that is because there is a good deal of extraneous technique about acting which can be taught, whereas the reading of poetry is a very subtle thing and almost incommunicable.

Tell a person to put feeling into his voice, and behold, he puts in sentimentality. Tell him to vary his voice with the different speakers, and he gives you a ventriloquistic effect which is horrible. The truth is, it is a question of the inch on the end of a man's nose. The slightest inflection awry and the whole effect is spoilt.

Speaking lines in a modern play is a comparatively easy thing; reading poetry is quite different. In a play, one can rely to a certain extent upon acting, and upon one's fellow actors. In reading, one is all alone, and one must not act. I do not mean that one should not read with expression. I mean that it is more dangerous to overdo dramatic expression than to underdo it.

Reading is not acting, and the point cannot be too strongly insisted upon. The pitfall of all elocution-taught readers is that they fail to see this distinction. Great actresses like Sarah Bernhardt or Duse do not make this mistake; it is the little people who are not sure of their power of creating an effect by an inflection who fall into the error.

Again, the reader must not be confused with the impersonator. Impersonators act out their parts, although they are all alone upon the stage. They are approaching the brains of their audiences from the same standpoint as the actor. They are acting, in fact.

This point is the crux of the situation. In a play, the audience is intended to see the march of events with its physical eyes. It is, as it were, looking through a window at an actual scene. It must be made to feel the reality of what is before it. Even in mystical plays like Maeterlinck's 'Pelléas and Mélisande' the audience must have the sense of actuality. Dream world though it be, it is for the moment real.

In reading, the impression to be made upon an audience is achieved by quite other means. Here the audience must see nothing with its eyes which detracts from its mental vision. It must be made to imagine so vividly that it forgets the reader in the thing read. The dramatic quality of the piece must be given just in so far as it stimulates imagination, but never so far as to call attention to the reader as an actual personality.

I have said that there is a good tradition of speaking poetry, and ninety and nine bad traditions. Let us consider for a moment the bad traditions. (I shall take the word 'reading' to imply the pronouncing of poetry aloud, whether it be done in character on the stage, or in *propria persona* from the platform.)

The first bad tradition is the mispronouncing of words. This starts from a misconception of the laws of English prosody, and a desire to heighten the poetical effect by some elegance other than those the author thought fit to insert.

The word most mispronounced in the whole vocabulary, by poetry readers and singers alike, is 'wind.' Unless the reader or singer is very well educated indeed, so well educated that he or she knows enough to be quite simple and natural, that unhappy word changes at once to 'winde.' Why? What is the reason for the change? The reason, in the case of nine readers out of ten, is merely that they have been taught to do it. But the reason which has actuated those teachers who have thought about the matter at all and not, themselves, repeated parrot-like from some earlier master, is based upon ignorance of the rules under which English poetry is written.

Why was 'wind' ever pronounced 'winde' in poetry, for it never is, and never was, in prose? Cannot we imagine the reason? Not a bad reason when one is in ignorance of any prosodic laws. It was because poets insisted upon rhyming it with 'find,' and 'bind,' and other words where the *i* was obviously long. To pronounce it with a long *i* saved the rhyming sound, thought these wiseacres, and that this pronunciation took all the windy

connotations away from the word was to them of
minor importance. Elocution teachers are seldom
concerned with *le mot juste*; 'winde' sounded like a
perfect rhyme, 'wind' did not, so 'winde' it had
to be.

But the good old English prosody which served
Shakespeare, and Spenser, and Milton so excel-
lently well, had one life-saving rule. It was that
words spelt the same and pronounced differently,
rhymed; as did also words pronounced the same
and spelt differently. For instance, 'plough'
rhymed with 'cow,' an obvious chime, as we have
recognized by spelling 'bough' with an 'ow' instead of the old 'ough'; also 'peak' rhymed with
'break,' and 'push' with 'rush,' and 'deaf' with
'sheaf.' All these non-chiming rhymes we have
kept, probably because of the difficulty of changing them to fit. For we all balk at the 'pake' of a
mountain, or at a brook 'rooshing' down a hill, and
few of us can 'pŭsh' ourselves to make such
radical changes. It is true that in old times 'deaf'
was universally pronounced 'deef,' but good use
has altered it to 'deaf' without altering its co-
rhymes, and he would be a bold man who should
dare to speak of a 'sheff' of wheat for any reason
whatsoever.

In recent years, a group of poetasters has arisen
who declare these near-rhymes to be an offence to

the ear, and they proudly eschew them — a reform
which would command more sympathy had these
precious gentlemen produced a single masterpiece
to substantiate it. They have not; and the reason
is not far to seek. The old, great masters knew
their job, and knew it superlatively well. They
realized that the English language suffers from a
paucity of rhymes. A certain elasticity was necessary if thought was to be adequately clothed in
metre and rhyme. Being artists, not pedants, they
found this elasticity, as I have shown.

Now we understand how 'wind' came to be
tortured into 'winde,' and can see why the latter is never under any circumstances to be employed.

An important rule for the reading of poetry is
never to mispronounce words. Give them the
sound they have in everyday speech, and let the
blunder of a false rhyme, if there be one, rest on
the author.

Another of the bad traditions insists that poetry
should be read as if it were prose. That is, that the
reader should follow the punctuation marks and
not the swing of the metre. This arose as a protest
to the equally bad tradition which dropped the
voice at the end of each line, regardless of the
sense. Of course, monotony was the result of this
latter practice. The sense of the poem was lost,

while the rhythm was exaggerated out of all proportion.

People have often taken issue with the proposition that poetry should not be read as if it were prose. People who have not grasped the meaning, that is. 'But,' they say, 'surely you don't like to have poetry read in a sing-song manner.' Assuredly, I do not; and yet I say, unhesitatingly, that if one must choose between these two bad traditions, I prefer to have the rhythm over-accented than to have it lost sight of altogether. As a matter of fact, neither extreme is necessary. The good tradition, as is the way with good traditions, seeks the happy mean.

Blank verse is a long, stately metre composed of simple, dignified feet. It is rare to find a blank-verse poem in which the rhythms should be more than faintly indicated. But there are other metres in which the effect is entirely lost unless the rhythm is brought out so strongly as to become almost a lilt. We must suppose that the poet knew what he was about when he chose one metre rather than another. It is an impertinence to obscure his rhythm, and not give it its full value.

But, it may be asked, how is one to know when a rhythm is to be merely indicated, and when it is to be actively stressed? I can only reply that much experience is required to know this. But experience is a sure guide. Knowledge of an author's methods, sympathy with the aim of the poem, a realization that certain metres require certain renderings, all these things tell the reader what he should do. In the last analysis, it is common sense, and nowhere is common sense more needed than in the reading of poetry.

Take the case of '*vers libre.*' For that to be misunderstood is both strange and unfortunate, since it owes its inception to no personal idiosyncrasy, but has been slowly evolved from existing laws. This is so little comprehended that hysterical people are constantly asking what it is, and whether it is prose or poetry, and is it destined entirely to supersede metrical verse.

To answer these questions categorically, let us begin with the last. Art has fashions; or if you prefer the term as more dignified, it is subject to the law of evolution. Differences are constantly being evolved; some are real changes, some only samenesses with a twist to them. Art, like life, has a queer way of revolving upon itself. Personally I feel that *vers libre* and metrical verse can exist side by side as cheerfully as do blank verse and quatrains. But this will not happen until people realize that *vers libre* is a prosodic form, and not an invitation to loose all the seven devils upon the reading public.

The second question, whether *vers libre* is poetry or prose, can be treated quite summarily. It is assuredly poetry. That it may dispense with rhyme, and must dispense with metre, does not affect its substance in the least. For no matter with what it dispenses, it retains that essential to all poetry: Rhythm.

Where stanzas are printed in an even pattern of metrical lines, some sense of rhythm can be gained by the eye. Where they are not, as in *vers libre*, the reading aloud becomes an absolute condition of comprehension. If the modern movement in poetry could be defined in a sentence, the truest thing which could be said of it, and which would include all its variations, would be that it is a movement to restore the audible quality to poetry, to insist upon it as a spoken art.

THE PROCESS OF MAKING POETRY

In answering the question, How are poems made? my instinctive answer is a flat 'I don't know.' It makes not the slightest difference that the question as asked me refers solely to my own poems, for I know as little of how they are made as I do of any one else's. What I do know about them is only a millionth part of what there must be to know. I meet them where they touch consciousness, and that is already a considerable distance along the road of evolution.

Whether poetry is the fusion of contradictory ideas, as Mr. Graves believes, or the result and relief of emotional irritation and tension, as Sara Teasdale puts it, or the yielding to a psychical state verging on day-dream, as Professor Prescott has written a whole book to prove, it is impossible for any one to state definitely. All I can confidently assert from my own experience is that it is not day-dream, but an entirely different psychic state and one peculiar to itself.

The truth is that there is a little mystery here, and no one is more conscious of it than the poet himself. Let us admit at once that a poet is something like a radio aërial — he is capable of receiving messages on waves of some sort; but he is more than an aërial, for he possesses the capacity of transmuting these messages into those patterns of words we call poems.

It would seem that a scientific definition of a poet might put it something like this: a man of an extraordinarily sensitive and active subconscious personality, fed by, and feeding, a non-resistant consciousness. A common phrase among poets is, 'It came to me.' So hackneyed has this become that one learns to suppress the expression with care, but really it is the best description I know of the conscious arrival of a poem.

Sometimes the external stimulus which has produced a poem is known or can be traced. It may be a sight, a sound, a thought, or an emotion. Sometimes the consciousness has no record of the initial impulse, which has either been forgotten or springs from a deep, unrealized memory. But whatever it is, emotion, apprehended or hidden, is a part of it, for only emotion can rouse the subconscious into action. How carefully and precisely the subconscious mind functions, I have often been a witness to in my own work. An idea will come into my head for no apparent reason; 'The Bronze Horses,' for instance. I registered the horses as a good subject for a poem; and, having so registered them, I consciously thought no more

about the matter. But what I had really done was
to drop my subject into the subconscious, much as
one drops a letter into the mail-box. Six months
later, the words of the poem began to come into
my head, the poem — to use my private vocabulary — was 'there.'

Some poets speak of hearing a voice speaking to
them, and say that they write almost to dictation.
I do not know whether my early scientific training
is responsible for my using a less picturesque vocabulary, or whether their process really differs
from mine. I do not hear a voice, but I do hear
words pronounced, only the pronouncing is tone-
less. The words seem to be pronounced in my
head, but with nobody speaking them. This is an
effect with which I am familiar, for I always *hear*
words even when I am reading to myself, and still
more when I am writing. In writing, I frequently
stop to read aloud what I have written, although
this is really hardly necessary, so clearly do the
words sound in my head.

The subconscious is, however, a most temperamental ally. Often he will strike work at some
critical point and not another word is to be got out
of him. Here is where the conscious training of the
poet comes in, for he must fill in what the subconscious has left, and fill it in as much in the key
of the rest as possible. Every long poem is sprin-

kled with these *lacunæ*; hence the innumerable rewritings which most poems undergo. Sometimes the sly subconscious partner will take pity on the struggling poet and return to his assistance; sometimes he will have nothing to do with that particular passage again. This is the reason that a poet must be both born and made. He must be born with a subconscious factory always working for him or he never can be a poet at all, and he must have knowledge and talent enough to 'putty' up his holes — to use Mr. Graves's expression. Let no one undervalue this process of puttying; it is a condition of good poetry. Of the many first manuscript drafts of great poets that have passed through my hands in the last twenty-five years, I have seen none without its share of putty, and the one of all most worked over is Keats's 'The Eve of St. Agnes.'

Long poems are apt to take months preparing in the subconscious mind; in the case of short poems, the period of subconscious gestation may be a day or an instant, or any time between. Suddenly words are there, and there with an imperious insistence which brooks no delay. They must be written down immediately or an acute suffering comes on, a distress almost physical, which is not relieved until the poem is given right of way. I never deny poems when they come; whatever I am doing, whatever I am writing, I lay it aside and attend to the arriving poem. I am so constituted that poems seldom come when I am out of doors, or actively engaged in company. But when I am alone, an idea contingent upon something I have seen or done when I am out will announce itself, quite as though it had been biding its time until it had me quiescent and receptive.

I seldom compose in my head. The first thing I do when I am conscious of the coming of a poem is to seek paper and pencil. It seems as though the simple gazing at a piece of blank paper hypnotized me into an awareness of the subconscious. For the same reason, I seldom correct poems while walking or driving; I find that the concentration needed for this is in the nature of trance (although that is too exaggerated a word for it), and must not be broken into by considerations of where I am going or what station I am to get out at.

This state of semi-trance is not surprising when we think of short poems; what is curious is that the trancelike state can hold over interruptions in the case of long poems. When a poem is so long that days or weeks are needed to write it, the mere sitting down to continue it produces the requisite frame of mind, which holds (except for the *lacunæ* I have spoken of) throughout its correction. On the other hand, no power will induce it if the subconscious is not ready; hence the sterile periods known to all poets.

I do believe that a poet should know all he can. No subject is alien to him, and the profounder his knowledge in any direction, the more depth will there be to his poetry. I believe he should be thoroughly grounded in both the old and the new poetic forms, but I am firmly convinced that he must never respect tradition above his intuitive self. Let him be sure of his own sincerity above all, let him bow to no public acclaim, however alluring, and then let him write with all courage what his subconscious mind suggests to him.

POETRY, IMAGINATION, AND EDUCATION

PERHAPS there never was a time when education received so much general attention as it does to-day. The world is deluged with books, pamphlets, and reviews on the subject, new systems are continually jostling the old out of place, new methods are constantly being applied, the very end and aim of education itself seems to change from time to time.

That the object of education should be to fit the child for life is such a trite and well-worn saying that people smile at its commonplaceness even while they agree with its obvious common sense. But the many ways of fitting the child, and the very various and diverse lives that have to be fitted for, are so perplexing that it is small wonder that curriculums multiply and still multiply their subjects in order to keep up with the complexity of modern existence.

More and more of late years has the old education by means of the humanities been broken down, and instead of it we see substituted a sort of vocational training. Children are now taught to do, where, in the older systems, they were taught to think. It is as if we had learnt to distrust what we cannot see, to demand an immediate tangible result for the outlay of preparation. This is perhaps largely due to our national temper. We are always in a hurry. But does this constant haste produce the results desired? 'Evolution, not revolution, is the order of development,' says Mr. Hughes, in his book on comparative education, and education is a process requiring much time. Nature cannot be hurried; there is no such thing as cramming possible to her methods. A congested curriculum results in the proper assimilation of no one subject, and what can we think of a primary school, boasting only one teacher, in which children were taught seventeen subjects, with fifteen minutes given to each subject, as was the case some years ago in a school which came under my observation.

No educator is so insensate as to approve of such a method, and it is just in the hope of simplifying education that this idea of dropping the humanities has been evolved. But, in considering the means as the end, to what are we led? What is the result of an over-insistence upon fact, and an under-emphasis upon the development of faculties? It is a result little realized for the most part; one which may fit in with the views of the more extreme socialists, perhaps, but hardly in accord with those rights of the individual which have always been America's brightest ideal. For it is precisely the humanities which develop individuality. A knowledge of facts does not make us men; it is the active use of brains which does that. Whatever tends to make the brain supple and self-reliant is a direct help to personality.

Perhaps the two qualities which more than any others go to the making of a strong personality are character and imagination. Character means courage, and there is a great difference between the collective courage of a mass of people all thinking the same way and the courage of a man who cares not at all for public opinion but follows his own chosen path unswervingly. Our national ideal as to the moral attitude is high; what the people understand, and what they all agree about, that they will do; but it is not so easy to find men who are willing to think and act at variance with the opinions of their neighbours. We see this trait constantly in those people who live beyond their incomes; who must have this and that because their friends have it. This weakness gnaws at the foundation of our national existence like an insidious disease. For, with all our talk of individualism, we are among the least individual of nations. The era of machine-made articles has swept over the land, and nowhere is its product more deteriorating than in the machine-made types which our schools turn out.

I do not wish to be misunderstood; I do not mean that these types are poor or bad types — on the contrary, machines work with a wonderful precision — but these types are run in a mould, or rather several moulds. The result is a high state of mediocrity. But there is a danger here which we do not quite foresee. Machines are controlled by the men who make and work them. Upon the few with the brains to create and guide, the destinies of the others therefore depend. There has never been such a machine-made people as the Germans; and we can see clearly to-day, as we could not some years ago, what happens to such a people when the guiding powers are unscrupulous and wrought upon by an overweening ambition.

A democracy can only succeed through an enlightened proletariat. If character and imagination are the essentials to a strong personality, one capable of directing itself and not at the mercy of demagogues and fanatics, then we should leave no stones unturned to gain this end. I think I make no unwise statement when I say that it is only in those minds possessing but a modicum of imagination that the value of the humanities as an educational factor is denied.

It is clearly not my purpose, in this paper, to speak of character building, neither have I space to go into all the ways in which the faculty of imagination might be stimulated, but there is one, and I think the most important one, the value of which is only imperfectly understood. I mean literature, and more especially poetry, and more especially still, contemporary poetry.

We all agree that the aim of education is to fit the child for life. But the differences of opinion as to how that fitting is to be done are almost as many as there are men to hold them. Again, we all agree as to the necessity of building up a strong character, but here again we are at variance as to how this is to be done. Still, upon these points the world is in accord; the point on which it differs radically is precisely that of imagination. Fully half of our pedagogues cannot see that imagination is the root of all civilization. Like love, it may very fairly be said to 'make the world go round.' But as it works out of sight, it is given very little credit for what it performs.

Pedagogy is being treated as a science, which would seem a start in the right direction, were it not that true science must be exact, mathematically so, and capable of being proved backwards. The slightest mistake in facts or reasoning throws the result hopelessly out.   Is it possible that, with all our scientific pretensions, we have overlooked a primary link in a logical chain? Is it possible that that link is the importance of the subconscious? Can it be said that the very lack of imagination in the pedagogic mind is responsible for this fatal error? But let us leap to no conclusions. Even if we think we see an end, let us not postulate upon it until we have reached it, step by step, and have proved its existence.

Character is no new thing in the world, neither is imagination, nor, indeed, education. Our ancestors were as much interested in these things as we are. Like us, they talked of character and education, and, like us, they did not talk of imagination. And yet I think it can easily be proved that their methods were more favourable to its development than our own.

Let us forget theories for the moment and take our stand upon an unassailable truism, namely that the object of education is to educate. Now, once more, forgetting the dusty cobwebs of twentieth-century discussion, let us consider the old dictionary definition of 'to educate,' which is 'to bring forth and form the natural faculties.' To bring forth and form the natural faculties, to bring out the best that the child has in him so that no talent nor power shall be left latent, and then so to train and cultivate these talents and powers

that the child shall obtain perfect control over
them, and make them of the fullest use.

Nothing is said here about fitting the child for
life. Our ancestors considered that so obvious a
fact as to need no stating, and this very reticence
proves an imaginative attitude which we seem to
have lost to-day.

It might be said quite truthfully that no one was
ever taught anything; that one learned, but was
not taught; that what the mind was ready for the
mind received, that what the mind was not ready
for fell away and was forgotten. Therefore the
true end of education as such must be to train the
mind. Another truism, you will say. Granted —
but how is this same training to be done?

The last generation believed in the old classical
education; they had forgotten why in many cases,
but the prejudice remained that Greek and Latin
were the best training. The reason was a perfectly
valid one: Greek and Latin were hard to learn and
needed brain application, also they could not be
learnt by rote; the boy had to use his mind and his
imagination, and, being accustomed to using his
mind and imagination in his studies, he brought
them to bear on other things as well.

We have not dropped the old classical education
entirely, but we have added many other things to
it, and in so doing have diminished the amount of

time and thought given to it, and consequently the amount of benefit to be derived from it. Of the things which we have added, some are really good, others appear so, but the total effect does not seem so very far in advance of the old method after all.

Our children are turned out with a smattering of many subjects, but can we say that they are any better educated than the men and women that preceded them? Are they better equipped for life? do they find the problems that they have to solve easier of solution? For there is one great fault in our educational systems to-day; they teach, but they do not train; and the one faculty without which no other can come to fruition is never really trained at all, for we cannot deny that imagination is forced to strive against adverse circumstances both at home and in school.

Years ago, before the education of little children was considered so important a subject as it is now, lessons were given in certain well-defined subjects; reading, writing, and ciphering (as it was then called) formed the staple of the school course, supplemented by geography, Latin, and, in the case of little girls, sewing.

Dreary enough these lessons must have been, for a-b, ab, many times repeated fails to germinate any interesting train of thought, and pot-hooks and hangers scrawled in interminable succession with a squeaky slate pencil on a slate leave the imagination cold.

But even if the lessons themselves were not in the least alluring, this same imagination was stimulated by the best of all methods, by the good old-fashioned fairy story; either told by some old nurse, or read out of enchanting books with innumerable quaint woodcuts, so that forever after the names of certain tales were inseparably bound up with the woodcuts in question, and to name the one was to see the other. There was no moral hidden away in these stories, except the wholesome one that the good always triumphed in the end; their aim was to amuse, to charm, and even sometimes to terrify, to beguile the child along the paths of unreality into the great and beautiful world of romance. Romance is a grasp of the ideal, an endeavour to express by symbols the great truths of life. Wedded to rhythm, it becomes poetry. It is the striving of the soul after the unattainable. And into this rich world the little child entered through the portals of the fairy story, as thousands of years before the nations in their childhood had entered; as the Nibelungen Lied, the Norse sagas, and the myths of every land are here to testify.

But to-day the fairy story is discountenanced,

or if the child is beguiled into reading a book purporting to be about a certain Jack Frost, a sprightly elf, he speedily discovers that he is really reading a treatise on the action of frost. One child's magazine absolutely forbids fairy stories, and in all, information, whether given outright or cleverly disguised as in the Jack Frost story, preponderates. This is a work-a-day world and solid information is at a premium. So we have 'Life in a Lighthouse,' 'Careers of Danger and Daring,' 'How a Big City is Lighted,' 'The Children's Room at the Smithsonian,' 'English Public Schools,' 'The Fairy Land of Science,' and many more articles and books, very informing, doubtless, but doubtless also very uninspiring.

These deal with the facts of life, and facts are most important things, but fancies are important too, and the fancies are not much cultivated to-day.

It is doubtful if fancy can be cultivated directly, it is too subtle and elusive, it must grow of itself, but conditions can be made conducive or the reverse. To be conducted through the realms of poetry and romance by a grown-up person, as one of a class of children all with differing needs and perceptions, at a given rate of speed, is not conducive to such growth.

To gain the greatest amount out of a book, one

must read it as inclination leads; some parts are to be hurried over quickly, others read slowly and many times over; the mind will take what it needs, and dwell upon it, and make it its own.

Its connotations are really what make a book of use in stimulating the imagination. As a musical note is richer the more overtones it has, so a book is richer the more it ramifies into trains of thought. But there must be time and space for the thought to develop; the reader must not be interrupted by impertinent comments and alien suggestions.

We all hate the poetry we learnt in school. Why? Is it because it was in school that we learnt it, or is it because the conditions were such that we never really learnt it at all, the fine inner sense of it and its beauty of expression were both hidden from us?

Children never know why a thing is beautiful, but if their taste has not been perverted they often feel that it is so. This feeling can be cultivated and improved until the time comes when the child can know why.

There are two ways in which books stimulate the imagination; one is by beauty of thought, the other is by beauty of form. It takes a much wiser head than a little child's to say why certain combinations of words are beautiful, but even a little child can feel their charm. A story well told and a story ill told are as the poles asunder. At first one might deny that a child could have artistic perception enough to notice the difference. But that would be merely to confuse with technical jargon. The primary test of good writing is really very simple. It consists in the effect produced. The well-told story will make the child thrill with delight, its scenes will be real to him, its people his own dear friends; the ill-told story will not keep his attention, and nothing in it will interest him much.

For the object of writing is to produce a given effect. The writing will be good according as the effect is produced or not. Simple actions are easily described; the old spelling-book did not need to be possessed of much literary ability when it told us that 'The boy is on the box,' but it was good writing as far as it went. From that to Shakespeare's poetry and Pater's prose is merely a question of degree. The effect is infinitely more subtle, more penetrating, but the words are equally adequate, and convey the meaning in the same succinct manner.

At first the child merely knows that this story or that story is interesting, that certain other stories are not interesting, he does not attempt to analyse why. Later he will make his first true criticism; he will say, 'It does not seem real,' or 'Nobody would do so.' He has detected bad writing; his imagination refuses to give credence to what its instinct declares not to be true. Gradually these criticisms of matter are added to by criticisms of form, and we have 'Nobody would talk like that.'

What makes the child think that nobody would do thus and so, or that nobody would talk in such and such a way? Partly his knowledge of life as he has lived it, of course. Though he has lived a very small life and his experiences have necessarily been few, yet through the life of his imagination he has been able to live much more, he has gained a conception of life far beyond anything that he has ever experienced.

If one can imagine oneself a child of twelve years old denuded of any knowledge or idea of anything except what he can have known or seen in his daily life, one will at once see how much more meagre his conceptions would be than is actually the case. Therefore what makes the child think that this or that thing that he is reading about is false is the knowledge that he has gained through his imagination.

The power of judgment is like water running up hill; water cannot rise higher than its own level, and judgment cannot go beyond the experience which informs it. To be sure that the judgment is sound, the school in which the experience is gained must be true to life. Only the best in literature and art is this, and it is with the best in literature and art that our children must be familiar.

There is a popular impression that so-called 'children's books' are the proper reading for children, and certainly very few children's books can be classed as belonging to the best in literature. But also the really great books are few in any literature, and there is much inspiration and profit to be got from books below this highest grade. Homer, Dante, and Shakespeare are like mountain-peaks, the horizon is wider on the heights, the air purer and more invigorating; but literature has its byways, and shady lanes, and quiet sequestered places as well, and because we enjoy mountain-climbing does not prove that there is no profit to be got in rambling through these simpler paths.

Many books purporting to be written for children are very good, have become classics, indeed; 'Alice in Wonderland,' 'Through the Looking-Glass,' George Macdonald's 'Princess and the Goblin,' and Thackeray's 'The Rose and the Ring' come under this class. But the mass of children's books are poor, with a poverty only varying in degree. This brings us to the question of whether children's reading should be confined to juvenile books.

The old argument that children do not understand grown-up books is really a groundless one. Some books written for older people are more enjoyed in childhood than they ever will be later. Longfellow's 'Hiawatha' is a good example of this, and in the case of many people it would be true also of the novels of both Scott and Dickens.

Even in cases where the full meaning is only faintly grasped, there is often much pleasure to be gained and consequently much profit. This is especially true of poetry. Children are often captivated by poetry which they cannot possibly understand, and the charm lies partly in the images it conjures up and partly in the music of the syllables; the main purport of the poem remaining forever concealed. But who shall say that this enjoyment in something so balanced and beautiful as a great poem has not a stimulating effect upon the imagination?

James Russell Lowell has told us that when he was a very little boy his sister used to read him to sleep with Spenser's 'Faery Queen.' It was the first poem he ever heard and he was very fond of it, but it was not until many years later that he discovered that it had a double meaning. How much his early intimacy with Spenser and other authors of the same class had in determining the extreme delicacy of his literary perception it is impossible to tell, but it is certain that it was not without effect.

It is always difficult to decide how much early environment has to do with later development, but all education is based on the belief that it has much to do with it, and one could cite instance after instance to prove this theory.

There is a remarkable example in the case of Charlotte Brontë. Her style has great vigour and beauty. It is exquisitely proportioned, quick, sure, and subtle. This seems extraordinary in the daughter of a poor country clergyman, whose nominal education was got at an inferior boarding-school, whose life was passed in a little country town, only varied by a few attempts at teaching as a governess in the country houses of richer families, and by one year and ten months in a pension in Brussels. But when we consider what her reading was as a child it does not seem so strange. In Mrs. Ward's introduction to 'Jane Eyre,' in the Haworth edition of Miss Brontë's novels, is the following passage: 'There were no children's books at Haworth Parsonage. The children were nourished upon the food of their elders: the Bible, Shakespeare, Addison, Johnson, Sheridan, Cowper for the past; Scott, Byron, Southey, Wordsworth, Coleridge, "Blackwood's Magazine," "Fraser's Magazine," and Leigh Hunt for the moderns; on a

constant supply of newspapers, Whig and Tory —
Charlotte once said to a friend that she had taken
an interest in politics since she was five years old;
on current biographies, such as Lockhart's "Life
of Burns," Moore's "Lives of Byron and Sheridan," Southey's "Nelson," Wolfe's "Remains";
and on miscellaneous readings of old Methodist
magazines, Mrs. Rowe's "Letters from the Dead
to the Living," the "British Essayists," collected
from the "Rambler," the "Mirror," and elsewhere, and stories from the "Lady's Magazine."
They breathed, therefore, as far as books were concerned, a bracing and stimulating air from the beginning. Nothing was softened or adapted for
them.'

It will be objected that Charlotte Brontë was a
genius, that her reading alone would never have
enabled her to write as she did. True; but even
genius needs to be trained!

But what has style to do with imagination, some
people will ask? Style has everything to do with
imagination. A really good style cannot exist without imagination. As the test of good writing is in
the effect produced, and the object of all writing
is to produce a given effect, so that effect must
be first clear to the mind of the writer, and this
requires imagination.

The writer conceives of his idea through the

power of imagination, and through the power of imagination the idea takes form again in the reader's mind; the vehicle of transmission is the writer's style. The more fully developed the imagination of both writer and reader, and the more adequate the style, the more perfectly transmitted is the idea.

Imagination is behind all the great things that have been said and done in the world. All the great discoveries, all the great reforms, they have all been imagined first. Not a poem has been written, not a sermon preached, not an invention perfected, but has been first conceived.

And yet imagination must take a second place to-day and give room for the learning of so-called *useful* things!

In a list of the books for boys and girls in a large public library near Boston, the subjects are divided under headings. 'Poetry' takes up only a part of one page out of a catalogue of twenty-nine pages; 'Fairy Tales and Folk-Lore' have another page, while one page and a half is devoted to 'Inventions and Occupations' and one page to 'Outdoor Life.' Of course some of the books that come under other headings, such as 'Famous Old Stories' and 'Other Countries,' are really good literature, but appallingly few. Leaving out those sections devoted to 'Younger Readers' and 'For

Older Boys and Girls,' that is, taking the middle
section which is especially adapted for children of
the grammar-school age, I find, out of a total of
four hundred and seven books, the only ones which
could be considered good literature are Aldrich's
'Story of a Bad Boy,' Defoe's 'Robinson Crusoe,'
Hughes's 'Tom Brown's School Days,' Steven-
son's 'Treasure Island,' Mark Twain's 'The
Prince and the Pauper,' Mary Mapes Dodge's
'Hans Brinker,' Kipling's 'Jungle Book,' Bunyan's
'Pilgrim's Progress,' 'Don Quixote,' Hawthorne's
'Wonder Book,' 'Tanglewood Tales,' and 'Grand-
father's Chair,' 'The Iliad' and 'The Odyssey,'
Irving's 'Rip Van Winkle' and 'The Legend of
Sleepy Hollow,' Malory's 'King Arthur,' Shake-
speare (the Ben Greet Edition), 'Gulliver's Trav-
els,' and Marryat's 'Masterman Ready' and
'Children of the New Forest.'

The poetry list is unaccountably inadequate,
consisting almost entirely of individual poems.
The only volumes listed are: Longfellow's 'Evan-
geline' and 'Hiawatha,' Macaulay's 'Lays of
Ancient Rome,' Scott's 'The Lady of the Lake'
and 'Marmion,' Stevenson's 'A Child's Garden of
Verses,' Tennyson's 'Idylls of the King,' and
Whittier's 'Snow-Bound.'

There are also collections of poetry, ten of
them, of which the best are Henley's 'Lyra He-

roica,' Lang's 'Blue Poetry Book,' and Lucas's 'Book of Verses for Children.'

The fairy-tale section is even worse, and how dreary the inclusion of the word 'Folklore' in a catalogue intended for the use of children. Certainly, the erudite person who made this selection never reads fairy stories for amusement. The pseudo-scientific flavour of 'folklore' has intrigued him sadly, else why include Kingsley's 'Greek Heroes' under 'Fairy Tales,' why entirely exclude Thackeray's 'The Rose and the Ring' and George Macdonald's 'Princess and the Goblin' and 'Princess and Curdie,' these last both better books than 'At the Back of the North Wind,' by the same author, which has been allowed? What is the matter with 'Through the Looking-Glass,' since 'Alice in Wonderland' is here, and here without the asterisk which tells the child that the library contains other books by the same author. Think of growing up conversant with only half of Alice! Where are the delightful fairy tales of Mrs. Molesworth? where are those of Perrault, of Lord Brabourne? and why are Andrew Lang's long series of coloured fairy books represented by only one, and again with no asterisk? Poor little children, at the mercy of such elders as this compiling gentleman!

The list for older boys and girls is somewhat better, and here we find 'Through the Looking-

Glass,' though why it should be considered too advanced for younger readers, I cannot imagine. But the fact that this older section starts out with Miss Addams's 'Twenty Years at Hull House,' is eloquent of the attitude of the present day. Alas for imagination, when the inclusion of such a volume in such a list is possible!

It is true, a child can have any book that the library contains by asking for it. But the children who frequent the library most belong to the poorer classes, and their only chance of becoming familiar with books out of school is at the Public Library. At home, they are not surrounded with a large culture which makes the names of the great writers household words to them. How do they know what to ask for? A catalogue tells them nothing, and the only shelves they have access to until they are eighteen are those containing the books in the list I have been quoting. And this is in a town famous for its educational system!

Probably the catalogues intended for the use of children in our large libraries would show conditions to be less unfortunate, but I think the one I have quoted is at least typical.

There is no education like self-education, and no stimulus to the imagination so good as that which it gives itself when allowed to roam through the pent-up stores of the world's imaginings at will.

There is a class of people known to all librarians as 'browsers.' They wander from shelf to shelf, now reading here, now there.   Sometimes dipping into ten books in the hour, sometimes absorbed in one for the whole day. If we look back to our childhood we shall see how large a part 'browsing' had in our education. One book suggested another, and as we finished one we knew the next that was waiting to be begun. They stretched on and on in a delightful and never-ending vista. The joy of those hours when we sat cross-legged on the floor, or perched on the top of a ladder, a new world hidden behind the covers of every book within reach, and perfect liberty to open the covers and enter at will, can never be forgotten.

We talk about 'creating a demand for books' among the children of the masses, and about 'giving them the reading habit,' and the best way to do this is to have a well-stocked reading-room of good books, books for grown-up people as well as for children, and let the children have free access to the shelves. They will be found reading strange things often, strange from the point of view of the grown-up person, that is. But in most cases their instincts will be good guides, and they will read what is best for them.

There is too much teaching to-day.

We love and admire certain things rather in

spite of what people say than because of it. We like to compare notes with some one who enjoys the same things that we do, but the real enjoyment was there before. Beauty cannot be proved as a mathematical problem can. If beauty is its own excuse for being, it is also its own teacher for perceiving. Contact with beautiful things creates a taste for the beautiful, if there is any taste to be created.

Not every one has a great deal of imagination, but every one has a certain amount capable of cultivation to a greater or lesser degree, and the chief stimulaters of imagination are the arts — poetry, music, painting; the humanities as opposed to the materialities.

The boy who said that his Shakespeare class was only questioned on the notes, and so, as the boys were pressed for time, they only read the notes, was giving the most eloquent testimony as to the absolute unfitness of his teacher. Doubtless the teacher would have been horrified had he known of this state of things, but his own imagination must have been very much in need of cultivating for him not to have noticed it.

For the last two years of my school course, I attended lectures on Shakespeare by an eminent Harvard professor. I remember those lectures very well; they made an indelible impression. We

learnt everything about the plays we studied except the things that mattered. Not a historical
allusion, not an antiquarian tit-bit, escaped us.
The plays were made mines of valueless information. Out of them we delved all sorts of stray and
curious facts which were as unimportant to
Shakespeare as to us. Not once in those two years
were we bidden to notice the poetry, not once was
there a single æsthetic analysis. The plays might
have been written in the baldest prose for all the
eminent professor seemed to care. They became
merely 'quaint and curious volumes of forgotten
lore,' and if what we learnt at those lectures were
a criterion, might indeed have been promptly and
satisfactorily forgotten. So much time and energy
had been wasted in finding out these things, and
when found out their proper goal was the bonfire.

In my own case, however, I was saved, saved
from the clutches of ignorant and unimaginative
Academia, by coming across a volume in my
father's library which opened a door that might
otherwise have always remained shut. Browsing
about one day, I found Leigh Hunt's 'Imagination
and Fancy.' I did not read it, I devoured it. I
read it over and over, and then I turned to the
works of the poets referred to, and tried to read
them by the light of the new æsthetic perception
I had learnt from Hunt.

So engulfed in this new pursuit was I, that I used to inveigle my schoolmates up to my room and read them long stretches of Shelley, and Keats, and Coleridge, and Beaumont and Fletcher. Guided by Hunt, I found a new Shakespeare, one of whom I had never dreamed, and so the plays were saved for me, and nothing was left of the professor's lectures except an immense bitterness for the lost time.

I have often thought that in this book of Leigh Hunt's we have an excellent text-book for what should be the proper teaching of literature, and especially of poetry. Poetry is an art, and to emphasize anything else in teaching it is to deny its true function.

The study of what is now called the 'science of æsthetics' is a difficult one. Such a book as Mr. Willard Huntington Wright's 'The Creative Will' is immensely stimulating to the artist, but would only be confusing to school-children, even to those of high-school grade. But much of this volume, much of the many volumes on the subject, could be expressed in simpler terms. Beginning by stimulating the child's artistic perceptions in the very primitive manner of the child's own re-actions, an example of which I mentioned earlier in this article, the teacher can easily inculcate certain rules and touchstones, enlarging upon them from year to year, and in this manner lay a firm foundation for literary understanding; for it is only through understanding that literature, and particularly poetry, can function as a direct stimulus to imagination.

I realize perfectly that this method would put a great strain on our teachers. It is comparatively easy to learn a series of antiquarian allusions and reel them off to a class; to analyse an æsthetic scheme is a much more difficult matter. I was interested to come across this very idea in an essay of Professor Dowden's which I read lately. But, having pointed out the difficulty, the wise professor ignored it, and proceeded to write his paper without the inclusion of a single æsthetic preoccupation. To be sure, he apologized for this in the preface, but the essay was published.

We see, therefore, that to permit poetry to exert its imaginative training upon youth, a complete change must take place in the method by which it is taught. We must lay aside the academic tricks of the trade. Our teachers and expounders must first put themselves to school; they must desert the easy path of historical anecdote, for the difficult one of æsthetic comprehension. They must teach their pupils what poetry is, and why it is good, greater, greatest. They must be enthusiastic pioneers for themselves and for their classes. They must forget the mass of criticism (most of it mischievous) grown up about the classics, and rediscover them with delight. An excellent way to begin would be to conduct a course upon living poets.

The most significant thing in America to-day is the popular demand for poetry. It has grown by leaps and bounds. I read recently in a newspaper that the demand for poetry at the training-camps was extraordinary. In the 'Book News Monthly' for July, is an interesting chart showing the increase in the publication of books on poetry and the drama since 1902. In that year, 220 such books were published in the United States; in 1916, there were 633. More volumes of this kind were issued than of any other kind except fiction, and fiction only exceeded by seventy-three volumes. The publication of fiction has markedly diminished of late years. Why? Simply because poetry is really much more vital than fiction. Once poetry had thrown off its shackles, once it had begun to speak freely, sturdily, with the voice of its own age, it found a ready audience. Even Academia is listening, puzzled a little perhaps, but still becoming daily more attentive. I have had various teachers tell me sadly that the difficulty in speaking of it to a class is that they do not know the good modern poetry from the bad, it is all so 'different.' What is the matter? What has happened to the critical faculty within the walls of learning? I am sorry to have to say it, but the answer is 'pure laziness.' It is so much easier to run through a couple of volumes of somebody else's conclusions and be guided by them, than to form one's own by first-hand contact with works of art. And then, too, it opens one to an awful danger. One may be wrong! Still, the world is growing, and humanists, no more than scientists, can afford to live in an intellectual back-water.

The humanities are not yet a dead letter; one cannot push out of place something which is daily proving itself an emotional force of profound importance. Granted that, as taught, they might as well go, so might science if it taught that the world was flat. Taught as they should be, imagination might once again assert its saving power over a materialistic world.

The printed outline of work for the English Department of one of our high schools begins with the following sentence: 'The primary aim during the first year is to read works of standard authors which, while quickening the imagination and presenting a strong element of interest, shall reinforce the History and the Latin.' Imagination in parenthesis, that is the attitude of education to-day! And until it is once more considered as worthy of being the end of a sentence and the end of an endeavour, education will not be the harmonious and nicely balanced thing that perfect development presupposes.

ON ELDER POETS

WALT WHITMAN AND THE
NEW POETRY

WHITMAN'S is a very curious case in the long line
of expressive geniuses. His message was given
entire in his first book, and for thirty years he
merely added to it. His was not a career of phases
in the literary meaning of that term. His first
phase, one of complete conformity and banality,
if we are to believe his contemporaries as well as
himself on the subject, was got over in the pages
of ephemeral journalism; he was already in his
second and final phase when he printed 'Leaves of
Grass' in 1855.

But, if his main attitude was invariable, his
practice underwent some modifications. For instance, in the matter of titles: I suppose no man
ever perpetrated worse titles than those in his
first volumes. He changed many of these later;
they became more literary, but less forceful, peculiar, original. 'Poem of the Road' is now 'Song
of the Open Road,' 'Broad-Axe Poem' is 'Song
of the Broad-Axe,' 'Poem of Salutation' attitudi-
nizes as 'Salut au Monde!' and 'Poem of Wonder
at the Resurrection of the Wheat' is diluted into

'This Compost.' Occasionally, however, he succeeded in making a possible new title. The awkward 'Poem of the Daily Work of the Workmen and Workwomen of These States' is shortened into 'A Song for Occupations'; and the 'Poem of the Sayers of the Words of the Earth' is not seriously injured by becoming 'A Song of the Rolling Earth.' Yet I think the very clumsiness of the early titles is intriguing, and the word 'song' has a painfully Victorian ring. Only rarely has he made an indubitable improvement. 'Poem of Many in One' is certainly better, if a trifle vague, as is 'By Blue Ontario's Shore,' and 'I Sing the Body Electric' was a burst of inspiration for which we must be grateful; it is hard to wish to read anything which announces itself as 'Poem of the Body.'

When his working over is followed into the text, the changes are usually happy. They are, on the whole, more effective and less brutal, or perhaps I mean vulgar; at any rate, less purely animal in connotation. The first stanza of 'Poem of the Body' begins:

The bodies of men and women engirth me, and I engirth them,
They will not let me off, nor I them, till I go with them, respond to them, love them.

In the later version this is changed to:

I sing the body electric,
The armies of those I love engirth me and I engirth
    them,
They will not let me off till I go with them, respond to
    them,
And discorrupt them, and charge them full with the
    charge of the soul.

✓ In other words, Walt Whitman's development
was a constant march towards a greater preoccupation with form. And here I wish to make a
statement which I fear will be somewhat startling.
I believe that Walt Whitman fell into his own
peculiar form through ignorance, and not, as is
commonly supposed, through a high sense of fitness; in this point he is at complete issue with the
moderns who are supposed to derive from him,
since they are perfectly conscious artists writing
in a medium not less carefully ordered because it is
based upon cadence and not upon metre. Whitman never had the slightest idea of what cadence
is, and I think it does not take much reading to
force the conviction that he had very little rhythmical sense.

Whitman was a great poet whether he invented
his form consciously or whether he stumbled into
it while endeavouring to avoid the obvious pitfalls
of an older practice; and that he was not what
Dr. Patterson would call 'aggressively rhythmic,'

I think I can, without much difficulty, show. I am perfectly aware that he has given reasons, and cogent reasons, for writing as he did in 'A Backward Glance o'er Travelled Roads,' but it is by these very utterances that I intend to prove my point.

First and foremost, Whitman was chiefly propagandist and only afterwards poet. He admits so much himself when he says: 'I say the profoundest service that poems or any other writings can do for their reader is not merely to satisfy the intellect, or supply something polish'd and interesting, nor even to depict great passions, or persons or events, but to fill him with vigorous and clean manliness, religiousness, and give him *good heart* as a radical possession and habit.'

That is merely a splendidly virile restatement of the Victorian theory that the chief end of art is a moral one. There is nothing in it which would not have met with the hearty accord of both Longfellow and Tennyson. For, after all, far-seeing though he was, Whitman was fundamentally of his age, and this odd fact confronts us again and again. It is true that, among modern poets, there is one group which holds somewhat to this opinion, but by far the most important poets believe art to be an entity, a saving entity, one which in itself contains the other, but nevertheless something of supreme value as it is. A work of art is not static, but dynamic. It carries within itself the power of growth and change. Its moral effect is not direct, but insidious and persistent.

A man does not love his wife because it improves his character to do so; he loves her because he must, his spiritual nature requires such functioning; but it is undeniable that the feeling serves a moral end as well. At moments Whitman dimly apprehended this, but generally his mind was of too harsh and primitive a texture to grasp it fully. He had a curiously limited way of viewing life principally from the outside: 'Whatever may have been the case in years gone by, the true use for the imaginative faculty of modern times is to give ultimate vivification to facts, to science, and to common lives, endowing them with the glows and glories and final illustriousness which belong to every real thing, and to real things only.' There is his vision, in the last line, and that is his bequest to the new world.

Whitman was like a prophet straying in a fog and shouting half-truths with a voice of great trumpets. He was seeking something, but he never knew quite what, and he never found it. He vanishes in the mist, and his words float back, dim, superb, to us behind him.

Whitman was artist enough, even in the beginning, to perceive that the type of verse current in his day would not fit the sublime and raucous message which meant poetry to him. He sought and sought, but what he reached was not through a process of creation, but through one of elimination. 'For grounds of "Leaves of Grass," as a poem, I abandon'd the conventional themes, which do not appear in it: none of the stock ornamentation, or choice plots of love or war, or high, exceptional personages of Old-World song; nothing, as I may say, for beauty's sake — no legend, or myth, or romance, nor euphemism, nor rhyme. But the broadest average of humanity and its identities in the now ripening Nineteenth Century, and especially in each of their countless examples and practical occupations in the United States to-day.'

One can imagine him being read centuries hence for his lists of occupations, much as we find Virgil's 'Georgics' greatly delightful for its catalogue of agricultural labours. But Virgil's catalogues are scarcely Whitman's. Those interminable bald statements of trades. Flat, flat, flat, seldom a pregnant word, scarcely a relieving gesture. In four hundred pages, I found so few, here they are:

Earth of the vitreous pour of the full moon, just tinged with blue!
O for the voices of animals — O for the swiftness and balance of fishes!

O for the dropping of raindrops in a song!
O for the sunshine and motion of waves in a song!

I do not say there are not others, only that I
have not found them. Beauty of another kind
there is, but just now I am speaking of the allevi-
ation of such passages as:

The usual routine, the work-shop, factory, yard, office,
    store, desk,
The jaunt of hunting or fishing, the life of hunting or
    fishing,
Pasture-life, foddering, milking, herding, all the person-
    nel and usages,
The plum-orchard, apple-orchard, gardening, seedlings,
    cuttings, flowers, vines...

This is by no means the beginning of the passage, and it continues uninterrupted for six pages!
The only hint at artistic selection in them is in
the assonance and alliteration of 'hinge, flange,
band, bolt' varying into the soft 'o' and changed
consonants of 'throttle.'

In the passage from 'A Backward Glance o'er
Travelled Roads' which I have just quoted, it will
be noticed that rhyme is considered a beauty and
eschewed. Nothing at all is said about rhythm,
but the inclusion of rhyme is significant, and bears
out my opinion that Whitman had a decided
liking for conventional verse although he did not
consider it an appropriate medium for what he

wanted to say. He was probably not among those who take to rhyme naturally, and so, being somewhat of a labor, it handicapped the pure expression of his thought, but I think he would have smiled considerably at the arrogant and one-idea'd young persons who condemn it wholesale. That he could rhyme, the first stanza of the 'Song of the Broad-Axe' proves:

Weapon shapely, naked, wan,
Head from the mother's bowels drawn,
Wooded flesh and metal bone, limb only one and lip
        only one,
Grey-blue leaf by red-heat grown, helve produced from
        a little seed sown,
Resting the grass amid and upon,
To be lean'd and to lean on.

A purist might object that there were a good many false rhymes in that passage, but let us not be purists, let us be people of taste and understanding. Now, if Whitman could write so fine a passage in rhyme, why does he think the use of rhyme improper to the bulk of his poetry? Frankly, flatly, unpedantically, because it was only occasionally that he could make rhyme 'go' as well as that. He was in the urgent haste of creation, the necessary rhyme stumbled and lagged, he must get on, the thought would not wait. So he got on; that is the long and short of the matter.

So much for Whitman's form and the cause of it. It sprang, not from a positive desire to give substance to a new conception of beauty, but from a negative one not to incorporate in his work any existing beauties whatsoever.

Here, at once, is a cleavage with the moderns. They are positively trying to do something; he is negatively trying not to do something else.

The layman is fond of calling all verse not based upon metre 'free verse.' It does not in the least trouble him that there is not, and cannot be, any such thing. The term is, obviously, derived from a mistaken translation of the French term *vers libre.* Now *vers*, in French, means line; and *vers libre* meant a line which was not obliged to contain a given number of feet. The true English equivalent would be 'free line,' but a better term is 'cadenced verse,' or a type of verse based upon cadence. We all know how difficult it is to correct terms already in current use. We grandiloquently employ the word 'hangar' to denote the building used to house a dirigible balloon, but a 'hangar' is simply a shed. Speak to nine people out of ten about a balloon shed, however, and they will gently set you right by assuring you that the technical name is 'hangar.'

So the term *vers libre* seems to be with us to stay, and it is most unfortunate. Still, I do not despair, we may succeed in pushing 'cadenced verse' to the front before long. But here is the point, cadence is rhythm. Modern *vers libre*, far from being non-rhythmical as some people have supposed, is entirely based upon rhythm. Its rhythms differ from those of metre by being less obvious and more subtle, but rhythm is, nevertheless, the very ground and root of its structure. *Vers libre* looks easy to write, and bad *vers libre* is easy; but when it is bad it is not *vers libre* at all, but prose cut into arbitrary lines. The lines of good *vers libre* are not arbitrary, they are determined by the interrelating circles of the rhythm. Every word is placed in relation to the whole, and a change of a syllable will often throw a line quite out, in absolutely the same way that a change of a syllable would throw out a line of metre.

Here is a point to be carefully considered and understood. Walt Whitman did not write in metre (I exclude for the moment his occasional metrical pieces), and neither did he write *vers libre*. What he did write was a highly emotional prose, rising at times into genuine rhythmical prose, the 'prose rhythmée' of our Gallic neighbours.

✓ His poems are true poetry, however, not only because of their essence, but because he approaches his subject from the poetic point of view. For what makes a literary work prose or poetry is not a matter of typography; it is a matter of approach and of return. By return I mean some device by which a poem is brought continually back to its starting-place — something which keeps the basic emotional symbol constantly reappearing throughout the poem. All nations have recognized this, and they have achieved this quality of return in diverse ways. Our own most usual form employs metre and rhyme, our Anglo-Saxon ancestors made use of alliteration, the Hebrews wrote in double images, the Chinese have a scheme of alternating tones which only their language could be capable of, the Japanese alternate lines of seven and five syllables, and so on. There are as many ways of achieving 'return' as there are prosodies, but in every one it is the determining factor of the technique of poetry. Now Whitman returns with a dominant thought, often with a specific set of words.

I am not going to labour the point. That what Whitman wrote was poetry, I think no longer admits of discussion, but that much of it had precious little rhythm is quite easily demonstrable. I am far from saying he never had it. There are superb instances to the contrary — for example, the lyric parts of 'Out of the Cradle Endlessly Rocking,' the whole poem 'Tears,' much of 'Passage to India' — and I think they are his finest work; but that he could have let so much pass which was quite innocent of any rhythmical pattern would seem to imply that he did not consider rhythm as of paramount importance. Again, he does not eschew rhythm with the other beauties, the conclusion being that he did not regard rhythm as a beauty.

Often and often I read in the daily, weekly, and monthly press, that the modern *vers libre* writers derive their form from Walt Whitman. As a matter of fact, most of them got it from the French Symbolist poets, they were nearest to our time; but, in spite of its French name, *vers libre* was written in England long before it was thought of in France; Milton wrote it in his choruses to 'Samson Agonistes,' Blake wrote it in various of the prophetic books, Matthew Arnold wrote it in 'The Nightingale,' Henley wrote it in 'London Voluntaries.' And all these poems are true *vers libre*, poems based upon cadence.

But why did not Whitman try this form instead of taking metrical verse as a base and dropping things out of it? I believe for two reasons: one was that he did not read, or like, these poems; the other, that he did not feel any vital urge towards rhythm. I believe that another reason for his poems taking the form they did was because of his habit of reading the heroic poems of Greece and Rome and Italy and the East in translations, and most of the translations of his day, with the exception of the Bible, were either in strict metre or in prose. Since he had cast out metre, heroic poetry in his mind unconsciously fell into the form of prose. Had he read Butcher and Lang's translation of Homer, or Waley's rendering of Chinese poems, he might have got a hint of cadence as a *genre* by itself, for he was quite capable of adopting modes of writing; he took things when they seemed to him suitable — like the Oriental return by repetition:

Houses and rooms are full of perfumes, the shelves are
    crowded with perfumes.

It would not take much knowledge of Oriental practice to get that. He might have found it in the 'Psalms' or 'Isaiah,' but it is on record that he had read translations of Eastern works. In 'Specimen Days' he quotes some lines from an old Hindu poem.

No, the moderns, even the modern practitioners of 'cadenced verse,' with the possible exception of Carl Sandburg, owe very little of their form to Whitman. What they do owe is an attitude, to determine which we must first consider what was this vision of the world that Whitman had. It is not difficult to find out. The whole of 'Leaves of Grass' shouts it to us, and he has also explained it in page after page of prose. He hands it to us like a nut wrapped in a shell. The shell is his speech — the nut? Well, as I have said, I doubt whether he himself had ever really seen it. Here is his brief, final summary:

'As long as the States continue to absorb and be dominated by the poetry of the Old World, and remain unsupplied with autochthonous song, to express, vitalize and give color to and define their material and political success, and minister to them distinctively, so long will they stop short of first-class Nationality and remain defective.'

Walt Whitman proposed to give them this autochthonous song. He would make a poetry of America, he would make it of the lives of the great even strata of work-people. He would include all activities, all trades, he would be the voice of the whole continent from coast to coast, he would be North, and South, and Middle, he would laud his country and believe in her; nothing should be beneath him, nothing above. It was a magnificent aim, and in great part he did exactly what he set out to do.

He saw that science had changed the face of the world; he knew that we must adjust. He believed in the poet's mission of seer. It was the poet who must proclaim not only the moment, but its future. He had read the words of a French critic who said that 'owing to the special tendency to science and its all-devouring force, poetry would cease to be read in fifty years.' He took up the challenge, and set himself to the task of refutation. He saw himself as America. In a curious, detached kind of way, he lifted himself, for purposes of expression, into the rôle of American superman. He took himself, and what he knew of America, and deified them into an ideal.

It was a great and noble thing to have some one sing for America, America as a base, a home land, not as a colony. The other poets of Whitman's day read far too much like colonials; only Lowell touched a native savour; the others, for all their Water-Fowls and Barbara Frietchies and Paul Reveres were (in a literary sense) directly sprung from British loins. We needed Whitman's message; we need it to-day. We need it as he meant it, rather than as he said it; much of it is in our blood, unnoticed but invigorating. But the letter of his speech — ah, there is the crux! Ill-digested, his message may be as dangerous as a Bolshevik pronunciamento. Walt Whitman was a law-abiding citizen, a bit of a dreamer, a grand, nebulous soul, a fine, intuitive poet. The last ignominy to him would be the usage of his words as pickaxes to tear down the governmental structure he loved. It is perhaps somewhat sadly significant that the three modern poets who most loudly acknowledge his leadership are all of recent foreign extraction. For the native breed is doing what? It is going back, back, slowly learning, seeing beauty as its ancestors saw it; following, not Whitman only, but Langland, and Chaucer, and Wordsworth, and Robert Burns, seeing beauty in to-day, their day; clinging to the fundamental human meanings which outlast mere tools and occasions. Is it time or Whitman that has caused us to cease our colonial habit? I believe both. Raw Whitman appeals to our late arrivals; modified Whitman is in us all.

Ah, but he was really American, the good grey poet; he not only dared the complete vision of his early manhood; later, when age had opened troubled vistas, he did not flinch from leaving a record of them: 'Modern science and democracy seem'd to be throwing out their challenge to poetry to put them in its statements in contradistinction to the songs and myths of the past. As I see it now (perhaps too late) I have unwittingly taken up that challenge and made an attempt at such statements — which I certainly would not assume to do now, knowing more clearly what it means.'

An inkling of his poetic lapses comes to him in old age also: 'I have probably not been afraid of careless touches from the first — and am not now — nor of parrot-like repetitions — nor platitudes and the commonplace. Perhaps I am too democratic for such avoidances.'

If that last sentence be true, democracy carries the coffin of art upon her shoulders. But I do not believe it. It is not by levelling down, but up, that democracy can ever succeed in adequately containing life. And even then, it will be with it as with the human race itself: the upward shoots thrusting above the even plane prove finally of the most importance.

Whitman was right when he declared that 'No one will get at my verses who insists upon viewing them as a literary performance, or attempt at such performance, or as aiming mainly toward art or æstheticism.' He has put it more succinctly in a poem:

. . . a book I have made,
The words of my book nothing, the drift of it every-
            thing.

His whole is more important than his parts. Some obscure feeling for fitness prompted him to put all his poems together, at the last, under his first generic title: 'Leaves of Grass.' His work was not

manifold, but single. It was all cut from one piece
— himself. But, after all, he wrote; and we to-day
also write. We have his poetic practice left to
examine. How did he treat his poems? how do we
treat ours?

In the first place, the modern has one frightful
bugbear, the *cliché*. It pursues him relentlessly,
and sometimes it catches him. Now, Whitman
says that he has not been afraid of platitudes nor
the commonplace. How very differently Mr. Sandburg manages his catalogues from the way that
Walt Whitman managed his! Here is a passage;
if you were to hear it without the slightest pos-
sibility of knowing who wrote it, in what particular pigeon-hole of literary history would you
place it, do you think?

Blow, trumpeter, free and clear, I follow thee,
Where at thy liquid prelude, glad, serene,
The fretting world, the streets, the noisy hours of the
    day withdraw,
A holy calm descends like dew upon me,
I walk in cool refreshing night the walks of Paradise,
I scent the grass, the moist air and the roses;
The song expands my numb'd imbonded spirit, thou
    freest, launchest me,
Floating and basking upon Heaven's lake.

I think that proves my contention that when
the prophet was off duty, the poet was very much
a man of his time.

And this prophet — Whitman is called the voice of his period, but here is a forward gaze which is almost uncanny:

I see not America only, not only Liberty's nation but
　　other nations preparing,
I see tremendous entrances and exits, new combinations,
　　the solidarity of races....
I see men marching and countermarching by swift
　　millions,
I see frontiers and boundaries of old aristocracies
　　broken,
I see the landmarks of European kings removed,
I see this day the People beginning their landmarks.

The extreme left wing of poetry might take those lines as a battle slogan were they unrelated to their whole. But the people in Whitman's eyes was no rapacious plunderer; it was a good quiet village folk, well able, because slow to conclude yet firm in conclusion, to govern itself. The poem goes on:

I see Freedom, completely arm'd and victorious and
　　very haughty, with Law on one side and Peace on
　　the other.

Law and Peace, but Whitman was no pacifist. Try as our literary aliens may to force him into the rôle of tutelary god to the conscientious objector, he resists. We should all know that he resisted, that he was bone and sinew of resistance in what he believed a righteous cause, if we read him instead of books about him. 'Drum-Taps' is scarcely the volume of a pacifist. And this man knew war. He followed the armies; in the hospital tents — the terrible hospitals of those days with practically no anæsthetics and no antiseptics at all — he saw suffering with naked eyes. He walked battlefields in the red sunsets of days of conflict:

Look down, fair moon, and bathe this scene,
Pour softly down night's nimbus floods on faces ghastly,
    swollen, purple,
On the dead on their backs with arms tossed wide,
Pour down your unstinted nimbus, sacred moon.

Reading this poem, we are instantly reminded of another poet who has seen war, Siegfried Sassoon. His book 'Counter-Attack' is full of just such scenes.

The modern poet is bitter. He has lost his old vision in the reek of war. He is not sad and merciful, he hates — hates the waste and useless horror of war. The setting-back of the clock of civilization is always in his consciousness. It is so with all the sincere writers of the present day. This consciousness of waste is minimized to Whitman by his far-seeing outlook of a present necessity. Besides, once more I reiterate that he was a man of his time. Not yet the day when dreamers dared proclaim their hope a possible reality. We are more self-conscious to-day. It may be a gain; it may be a loss; but it is a fact. Besides, not in all the ranks of modern poetry has there yet appeared a seer.

Was Whitman's vision a true one? This America which he so loved, has she that within her through which she can rise victorious above all catastrophes? It is all in his poem 'Thou Mother with thy Equal Brood':

In many a smiling mask death shall approach beguiling
    thee, thou in disease shalt swelter,
The livid cancer spread its hideous claws, clinging upon
    thy breasts, seeking to strike deep within,
Consumption of the worst, moral consumption, shall
    rouge thy face with hectic,
But thou shalt face thy fortunes, thy diseases, and sur-
    mount them all.

He could write so because it was only a vision. In security he could gaze clear-eyed at chaos, for the future has its perspective as well as the past. Do not expect such utterance from modern poets. The disease is here; haply we may preserve our sanity. To keep on going, to see beauty still beyond the red night, that is the awful task before our poets to-day. Granted that all are not worthy to be taken seriously, why, every age has had this same difficulty — clouds of gnats buzzing about

the falcons. But gnats are short-lived creatures,
while the falcons endure. It is confusing; but
make no mistake, it has always been confusing.

Whitman is not always on the mountain-peak
of prophecy. Sometimes he is unexpectedly the
poet of pure beauty. Nothing could be more
modern, nothing more akin to the point of view
of our contemporaries, than this:

To me every hour of the light and dark is a miracle,
Every inch of space is a miracle,
Every square yard of the surface of the earth is spread
    with the same,
Every foot of the interior swarms with the same;
Every spear of grass — the frames, limbs, organs, of
    men and women, and all that concerns them,
All these to me are unspeakably perfect miracles.

And this is the very essence of that type of
poetry which we have learnt to call Imagistic:

Through the ample open door of the peaceful country
    barn,
A sunlit pasture field with cattle and horses feeding,
A haze and vista, and the far horizon fading away.

There are many such pictures: 'Cavalry Cross-
ing a Ford,' 'Bivouac on a Mountain Side,' 'An
Army Corps on the March,' and others; yet it
would be utter folly to consider that the vignettes
in modern work derive from Whitman, when, in
his own day, this sort of thing was being done,

and much better done, by Emily Dickinson. In almost all such cases, the moderns have found their prototype elsewhere than in Whitman, although it is undeniable that Whitman hints at many of the ways of modern practice. 'Away with love verses sugar'd in rhyme' might be taken as a slogan by some of our younger lyrists. 'The indirect is just as much as the direct' has a sympathetic sound to various of our present-day groups, and Whitman calls this indirectness 'Suggestiveness.' The modern term scarcely differs, it is 'Suggestion.' He analyses it exactly as we do: 'I round and finish little, if anything; and could not, consistently with my scheme. The reader will always have his or her part to do, just as much as I have had mine. I seek less to state or display any theme or thought, and more to bring you, reader, into the atmosphere of the theme or thought — there to pursue your own flight.' Yet how far Whitman was from the indirectness of present-day methods!

To compare what is near and yet very far is always a delightful occupation. Here are two poems built upon almost the same theme. One is Whitman's 'O Magnet-South.'

O magnet-South! O glistening perfumed South! my South!
O quick metal, rich blood, impulse and love! good and evil, O all dear to me!

O dear to me my birth-things — all moving things and
　　　the trees where I was born — the grains, plants,
　　　rivers,
Dear to me my own slow sluggish rivers where they flow,
　　　distant over flats of silvery sands or through
　　　swamps,
Dear to me the Roanoke, the Savannah, the Altamahaw,
　　　the Pedee, the Tombigbee, the Santee, the Coosa
　　　and the Sabine,
O pensive, far away wandering, I return with my soul
　　　to haunt their banks again.

This is from Carl Sandburg's 'Prairie':

I was born on the prairie and the milk of its wheat, the
　　　red of its clover, the eyes of its women, gave me
　　　a song and a slogan.
Here the water went down, the icebergs slid with gravel,
　　　the gaps and the valleys hissed, the black loam
　　　came, and the yellow sandy loam,
Here between the sheds of the Rocky Mountains and
　　　the Appalachians, here now a morning star fixes
　　　a fire sign over the timber claims and cow
　　　pastures, the corn belt, the cotton belt, the cattle
　　　ranches.
Here the gray geese go five hundred miles and back
　　　with a wind under their wings honking the cry
　　　for a new home.
Here I know I will hanker after nothing so much as one
　　　more sunrise or a sky moon of fire doubled to a
　　　river moon of water.
The prairie sings to me in the forenoon and I know in the
　　　night I rest easy in the prairie arms, on the
　　　prairie heart.

Both those passages are mere fragments of the poems to which they belong, but they show a great deal. For instance, the sentimentality which underlay Whitman's coarseness; the complete absence of it in Sandburg. It is the difference of sixty years. The world is no longer the same.

I might make more of these comparisons. For instance, 'The Song of the Redwood Tree' with Vachel Lindsay's 'Golden Whales of California,' although, to be sure, the latter is ironical; or, again, Whitman's group of poems about Lincoln, with John Gould Fletcher's 'Abraham Lincoln,' by far the finest modern poem on the subject. Since I may not do this, I must content myself with citing a few differences. I have mentioned the modern horror of the *cliché*. Another nightmare is the inversion; but so far removed from our point of view was Whitman, that he could calmly produce this very type and model of the dreadful thing:

O little shells, so curious-convolute, so limpid, cold and voiceless,
Will you not little shells to the tympans of temples held,
Murmurs and echoes still call up, eternity's music faint and far.

Whitman, like all poets, felt a pleasure in mere words, and particularly, it would seem, in foreign words. They are a constant source of misery in reading him, for his use of them is frequently ill judged. One thing is very marked to-day: a large number of the poets are fair linguists. I think scarcely one of them could be guilty of such an amazing grammatical blunder as the following:

> Now I absorb immortality and peace,
> I admire death and test proportions.
> How plenteous! how spiritual! how résumé!

It is dangerous to use foreign words when you do not even know whether they are parts of verbs, or nouns, or adjectives. Even in his own tongue what can one think of the taste which would perpetrate such a line as 'The rich man's elegant villa'!

That kind of thing could not find a lodgment anywhere in print now, but it was rife in Whitman's day, and Whitman was — he was several things — a great voice, and a silly, flattered old man; a conceited, ardent young fellow spattered with genius, and a primitive being teased by violent animal reactions. He was a powerful original poet, with a somewhat disconcerting dash of the poseur. Singer, prophet, orator, lover of beauty, sentimentalist, and often slovenly workman, his poems are that splendid paradox — himself. Magnificence punctuated with 'the things no fellow can do'; in substance, technique, fact, it is the same. To follow him is merely to imitate the pattern of his cloak. His time is past; we have ours. It is (to use the sort of language affected by his closest imitators) 'up to us.' Let us be thankful for him as we are thankful for Theocritus, and Dante, and Chaucer, and Browning. But our skies are not his, and he would be the first to wish us 'God speed' under them. Has he not written: 'Let me not dare, here or anywhere, for my own purposes, or for any purposes, to attempt the definition of Poetry, nor answer the question what it is. Like Religion, Love, Nature, while those terms are indispensable, and we all give a sufficiently accurate meaning to them, in my opinion no definition that has ever been made sufficiently encloses the name Poetry; nor can any rule or convention ever so absolutely obtain but some great exception may arise and disregard and overturn it.'

Sane and wise words, but indeed the writing of books is dust unless we can also say with him:

> Camarado, this is no book,
> Who touches this touches a man.

EMILY DICKINSON

I wonder what made Emily Dickinson as she was. She cannot be accounted for by any trick of ancestry or early influence. She was the daughter of a long line of worthy people; her father, who was the leading lawyer of Amherst, Massachusetts, and the treasurer of Amherst College, is typical of the aims and accomplishments of the race. Into this well-ordered, high-minded, average, and rather sombre milieu, swept Emily Dickinson like a beautiful, stray butterfly, 'beating in the void her luminous wings in vain.' She knew no different life; and yet she certainly did not belong to the one in which she found herself. She may have felt this in some obscure fashion; for, little by little, she withdrew from the world about her, and shut herself up in a cocoon of her own spinning. She had no heart to fight; she never knew that a battle was on and that she had been selected for a place in the vanguard; all she could do was to retire, to hide her wounds, to carry out her little skirmishings and advances in byways and side-tracks, slowly winning a territory which the enemy took no trouble to dispute. What she did seemed insignificant and individual, but thirty years after her death the flag under which she fought had become a great banner, the symbol of a militant revolt. It is an odd story, this history of Imagism, and perhaps the oddest and saddest moment in it is comprised in the struggle of this one brave, fearful, and unflinching woman.

There is very little to tell about Emily Dickinson's life. In a sense, she had no life except that of the imagination. Born in Amherst in December, 1830, she died there in May, 1886. Her travels consisted of occasional trips to Boston, and one short sojourn in Washington during her father's term in Congress. As the years went on, she could scarcely be induced to leave her own threshold; what she saw from her window, what she read in her books, were her only external *stimuli*. Those few people whom she admitted to her friendship were loved with the terrible and morbid exaggeration of the profoundly lonely. In this isolation, all resilience to the blows of illness and death was atrophied. She could not take up her life again because there was no life to take. Her thoughts came to be more and more preoccupied with the grave. Her letters were painful reading indeed to the normal-minded. Here was a woman with a nice wit, a sparkling sense of humour, sinking under the weight of an introverted imagination to a state bordering upon neurasthenia; for her horror of publicity would now certainly be classed as a 'phobia.' The ignorance and unwisdom of her friends confused illness with genius, and, reversing the usual experience in such cases, they saw in the morbidness of hysteria, the sensitiveness of a peculiarly artistic nature. In the introduction to the collection of her letters, the editor, Mrs. Mabel Loomis Todd, says, 'In her later years, Emily Dickinson rarely addressed the envelopes; it seemed as if her sensitive nature shrank from the publicity which even her handwriting would undergo, in the observation of indifferent eyes. Various expedients were resorted to — obliging friends frequently performed this office for her; sometimes a printed newspaper label was pasted upon the envelope; but the actual strokes of her own pencil were, so far as possible, reserved exclusively for friendly eyes.'

That is no matter for laughter, but for weeping. What loneliness, disappointment, misunderstanding must have preceded it! What unwise protection against the clear, buffeting winds of life must have been exerted to shut the poor soul into her stifling hot-house! The times were out of joint for Emily Dickinson. Her circle loved her, but utterly failed to comprehend. Her daring utterances shocked; her whimsicality dazed. The account of this narrow life is heart-rending. Think

of Charles Lamb joking a New England deacon;
imagine Keats's letters read aloud to a Dorcas
Society; conceive of William Blake sending the
'Songs of Experience' to the 'Springfield Repub-
lican'! Emily Dickinson lived in an atmosphere
of sermons, church sociables, and county newspapers. It is ghastly, the terrible, inexorable
waste of Nature, but it is a fact. The direct descendant of Blake (although she probably never
heard of him) lived in this surrounding. The
marvel is that her mind did not give way. It did
not; except in so far as her increasing shrinking
from society and her preoccupation with death
may be considered giving way. She lived on; she
never ceased to write; and the torture which she
suffered must have been exquisite indeed.

Whenever a little door opened, some kind friend
immediately slammed it to. Her old school com-
panion Mrs. Jackson, better known as H. H., the
author of 'Ramona,' repeatedly begged her to
write for the 'No Name Series,' then just starting.
And the poet whom everybody deemed so retiring
was half inclined to accept. She needed to be
pushed into the healthy arena of publicity, a little
assistance over the bump of her own shyness and
a new, bright, and vigorous life would have lain
before her. In an evil moment she asked the
advice of Mr. Thomas Wentworth Higginson. The

very words of her letter show her half pleading to be urged on:

DEAR FRIEND:

Are you willing to tell me what is right? Mrs. Jackson, of Colorado, was with me a few moments this week, and wished me to write for this. I told her I was unwilling, and she asked me why? I said I was incapable, and she seemed not to believe me and asked me not to decide for a few days. Meantime she would write to me.... I would regret to estrange her, and if you would be willing to give me a note saying you disapproved it and thought me unfit, she would believe you.

The disapproval was cordially given; the door shut again upon the prisoner, who thanks her jailor with the least hint of regret between the lines:

DEAR FRIEND:

... I am glad I did as you would like. The degradation to displease you, I hope I may never incur.

Mild, sweet-tempered, sympathetic, and stupid Mr. Higginson! It was an evil moment when Emily chose him for the arbiter of her fate. And yet who, at the time, would have done better? Certainly not Longfellow, nor Lowell, nor Emerson. Poe? But Emily could not write to a man like Poe. Whitman? She herself says in another letter to her mentor, 'You speak of Mr. Whitman. I never read his book, but was told that it was disgraceful.'

No, there was no hope. All her friends were in the conspiracy of silence. They could not believe that the public was made up of many people as sensitive as themselves. Mrs. Gordon L. Ford has related an interesting anecdote illustrative of this point of view. I will give it in her own words:

Dr. Holland once said to me, 'Her poems are too ethereal for publication.' I replied, 'They are beautiful — so concentrated — but they remind me of air-plants that have no roots in earth.' 'That is true,' he said, 'a perfect description;' and I think these lyrical ejaculations, these breathed-out projectiles, sharp as lances, would at that time have fallen into idle ears.

And yet when her first volume was published posthumously, it went through six editions in as many months.

The truth is that, as some one once said to me, the average man is a good deal above the average. A fact which the newly awakened interest in poetry is proving every day. This same first edition was published in 1890, more than twenty years before Imagism as a distinct school was heard of, but its reception shows that the soil was already ripe for sowing.

They bothered the critics dreadfully, these original, impossible poems, where form (conventional form) was utterly disregarded, but where somehow effects were got surprisingly well without it. Mr. Higginson shuddered and admired in about equal proportions, but he comes out nobly in praise (with reservations) in the preface to the first edition. His praise shows more discrimination than one would expect; his reservations are those proper to the time and the person. Addressing the 'thoughtful reader' (O, age of apologies and bombast!) he trusts that this judicious person 'will find in these pages a quality more suggestive of the poetry of William Blake than of anything to be elsewhere found — flashes of wholly original and profound insight into nature and life; words and phrases exhibiting an extraordinary vividness of descriptive and imaginative power, yet often set in a seemingly whimsical or rugged frame.'

The 'ruggedness' consists in the rhymes being frequently ignored. Mr. Higginson has himself told us how stiff in her own convictions the docile Emily became when he tried to improve the technique of her poems. To him, her practice was a lapse from the only true way, and he wondered at the firmness with which she held to her own method:

Though curiously indifferent to all conventional rules, [she] had a rigorous literary standard of her own, and often altered a word many times to suit an ear which had its own tenacious fastidiousness.

Mrs. Todd is more understanding. She probably

had had a less exacting classical education, and possessed a less prejudiced and more musical ear. In an explanatory passage in the volume of letters, she says: 'They [her verses] are pervaded by a singular cadence of hidden rhythmical music, which becomes sympathetically familiar upon intimate acquaintance.' And again in the preface to the second series of poems: 'In Emily Dickinson's exacting hands, the especial, intrinsic fitness of a particular order of words might not be sacrificed to anything virtually extrinsic; and her verses all show a strange cadence of inner rhythmical music. Lines are always daringly constructed, and the "thought-rhyme" appears frequently — appealing, indeed, to an unrecognized sense more elusive than hearing.'

Exactly what Mrs. Todd means by 'thought-rhyme,' I do not know. Perhaps she means a return of the idea, perhaps she merely means assonance, a compromise which Emily often substituted for true rhyme.

Thanks to Mr. Higginson, some of my work has already been done for me. He has told us that this is a poetry of 'flashes,' therefore it must be extremely concentrated; he says that it is wholly original, so it must give free rein to individualistic freedom of idea; he thinks that it exhibits 'an extraordinary vividness of description and imaginative power,' which is merely to restate the third and fourth Imagist canons in other words. His very objection to its rugged character proves that it occupies itself with new rhythms. What else is left? Simplicity and directness of speech, perhaps. For that, we had better seek our answer in the poems themselves, remembering that Mrs. Todd specifically says that 'a particular order of words might not be sacrificed to anything virtually extrinsic.'

In 'The Single Hound,' the fourth and last[1] volume of her work, issued in 1914 by her niece, is this poem, No. LXVI. Emily seldom gave her poems titles. Most of the titles in the first three volumes were added by Mr. Higginson and Mrs. Todd.

LXVI

A prompt, executive Bird is the Jay,
Bold as a Bailiff's hymn,
Brittle and brief in quality —
Warrant in every line;
Sitting a bough like a Brigadier,
Confident and straight,
Much is the mien
Of him in March
As a Magistrate.

---

[1] [This volume is no longer the last. *Further Poems of Emily Dickinson* was published in 1929.]

I can easily imagine that the language in that poem might have struck Mr. Higginson as 'rugged.' Anything more racy and forthright it would be hard to conceive. The speech of her letters is often sentimental and effeminate; the speech of her poems is almost without exception strong, direct, and almost masculine in its vigour. This, No. XLII, in 'The Single Hound,' has that acid quality of biting satire which we remarked in Blake's 'Songs of Experience':

XLII

The butterfly obtains
But little sympathy,
Though favourably mentioned
In Entomology.
Because he travels freely
And wears a proper coat,
The circumspect are certain
That he is dissolute.
Had he the homely scutcheon of modest Industry,
'Twere fitter certifying for Immortality.

Emily Dickinson had the divine gift of start-lingly original expression. Her letters are full of such 'flashes' as:

I love those little green ones [snakes] that slide around by your shoes in the grass, and make it rustle with their elbows.

The wind blows gay to-day and the jays bark like blue terriers.

The lawn is full of south and the odours tangle, and I hear to-day for the first the river in the tree.

The moon rides like a girl through a topaz town.

And, in a description of a thunderstorm:

> The leaves unhooked themselves from trees
> And started all abroad;
> The dust did scoop itself like hands
> And throw away the road.

Her sense of sound was extraordinarily acute, for instance the droning of this:

> Like trains of cars on tracks of plush
> I hear the level bee:
> A jar across the flower goes.

The following might be said to be the inaudible but realized sound of an overwhelming burst of bright light:

> ... mornings blossom into noons
> And split their pods of flame.

She has something of Coleridge's feeling for the sound connotations of words, in one place she says:

> An awful tempest mashed the air.

Down from Blake through Coleridge, that is Emily Dickinson's line of descent. Here is something of the fantastic quality of 'The Ancient Mariner,' and the true Coleridge use of colour:

VII

When Etna basks and purrs,
Naples is more afraid
Than when she shows her Garnet Tooth;
Security is loud.

No poet ever revelled more in his own imagination than did this one. She flies her kite with infinite satisfaction to herself and to us. Over poor little Amherst it goes, tipping and veering, and her friends, intrigued but not wholly at ease in the sight, beg her not to let the neighbours see. This poem was sent with a nosegay of brilliant flowers:

LV

I send two Sunsets —
Day and I in competition ran,
I finished two, and several stars,
While He was making one.

His own is ampler —
But, as I was saying to a friend,
Mine is the more convenient
To carry in the hand.

Here is one in which she half piteously, half
bitterly refers to her own obsession by the thought
of death:

LIII

> The long sigh of the Frog
> Upon a Summer's day,
> Enacts intoxication
> Upon the revery.
> But his receding swell
> Substantiates a peace,
> That makes the ear inordinate
> For corporal release.

Religion is an attitude of the spirit, and no one
was ever more innately, positively religious than
Emily Dickinson. But the cramped religion of
orthodox New England repelled her in spite of her
training. Her family and friends recognized this
dimly, but too dimly not to feel that the point of
view needed a kindly cloak. In the Preface to the
'Letters,' Mrs. Todd explains and explains: 'To
her, God was not a far-away and dreary Power
to be daily addressed — the great "Eclipse of
which she wrote — but He was near and familiar
and pervasive. Her garden was full of His bright-
ness and glory; the birds sang and the sky glowed
because of Him. To shut herself out of the sunshine in a church, dark, chilly, restricted, was
rather to shut herself away from Him; almost pa-

thetically she wrote, "I believe the love of God may be taught not to seem like bears." In essence, no real irreverence mars her poems or her letters.'

Was that necessary? Perhaps it was at the time, although I hardly think so; it certainly is not now. And for that very reason this little volume, 'The Single Hound,' is worth the other three volumes put together. One cannot help feeling that the editors of the first three series compiled the books with an eye to conciliating criticism. The whole of Emily is not in them, as it is in 'The Single Hound'; in fact, the most interesting part of her genius suffers eclipse at the hands of her timorous interpreters. Yet even in the first collection there are poems which reveal the whole tragedy of her life, poems which must have wounded her survivors if they really understood them, which must have shocked some sensibilities by the sheer brutality of their truth.

Book IV

X

I died for beauty, but was scarce
Adjusted in the tomb,
When one who died for truth **was lain**
In an adjoining room.

He questioned softly why I failed.
'For beauty,' I replied.

'And I for truth, — the two are one;
We brethren are,' he said.

And so, as kinsmen met a night,
We talked between the rooms,
Until the moss had reached our lips,
And covered up our names.

Her whimsicality is very refreshing. It is not only in thought, but in expression:

XXX

I bet with every Wind that blew, till Nature in chagrin
Employed a *Fact* to visit me and scuttle my Balloon!

Now notice the next to last line of this poem, and see if it is not complete Imagism:

XXXVIII

A little madness in the Spring
Is wholesome even for the King,
But God be with the Clown,
Who ponders this tremendous scene —
This whole experiment of green,
As if it were his own!

'This whole experiment of green!' Why, to read that is to see the little-leaved May world, all broken out in light, jocund verdure, such as happens at no other time of the year!

The exact word, the perfect image, that is what

makes these short poems so telling. Take this picture:

LXVII

> Like brooms of steel
> The Snow and Wind
> Had swept the Winter Street,
> The House was hooked,
> The Sun sent out
> Faint Deputies of heat —
> Where rode the Bird
> The Silence tied
> His ample, plodding Steed,
> The Apple in the cellar snug
> Was all the one that played.

Here is a stanza describing the wriggling forward of a snake. Forget the involutions of the words, and notice only the movement contained in them:

> Then, to a rhythm slim
> Secreted in his form,
> As patterns swim,
> Projected him.

If we were to arrange those words in a more usual order, should we get the sinuosity of the snake's advance? I doubt it.

Emily Dickinson is a master in the art of presenting movement. In another poem, she gives all the collateral effects of a snake squirming through grass so poignantly that, as one reads it,

one involuntarily looks down at one's feet with a
shudder:

> The grass divides as with a comb,
> A spotted shaft is seen;
> And then it closes at your feet
> And opens further on.

Those lines illustrate very aptly the 'ruggedness' which so troubled Mr. Higginson. 'Seen'
does not rhyme with 'on,' the two words do not
even make an assonance; we have only the two *n*'s
and the long *e* against the *o* to help the ear to a
kind of return. Yet return is here; and that the
poet sought for it is quite evident. She would not
sacrifice the *exact* word for a rhyme, but she must
round her circle somehow.

Emily Dickinson was not one of those poets
who rhyme by nature. The necessity for rhyming
evidently bothered her. She had no conscious idea
of any form of verse not built upon metre. All
the poetry with which she was familiar was
metrical and rhymed. She tried to tie her genius
down to the pattern and signally failed. But she
was too much of an artist to cramp herself beyond
a certain point. When what she wanted to say
clashed with her ability to rhyme, the rhymes
went to the wall. In the following poem, she evidently intended to rhyme the second and fourth
lines of each stanza, but the words were stubborn,

the idea exacting; the result is that there is not a single rhyme throughout, only so many subterfuges, ingenious enough, but a begging of the issue after all.

THE SAINTS' REST

Of tribulation these are they,
　　Denoted by the white;
The spangled gowns, a lesser rank
　　Of victors designate.

All these did conquer; but the ones
　　Who overcame most times,
Wear nothing commoner than snow,
　　No ornaments but palms.

'Surrender' is a sort unknown
　　On this superior soil;
'Defeat,' an outgrown anguish,
　　Remembered as the mile

Our panting ankle barely gained
　　When night devoured the road;
But we stood whispering in the house,
　　And all we said was 'Saved!'

I have said that Emily Dickinson had no conscious idea of any form of verse other than the metrical. She does not seem to have known Blake at all, and if she read Matthew Arnold, or Henley, she made no happy discovery of their use of *vers libre*. The poetry she knew was in metre, and she did her best to cram her subtle rhythmic sense into a figure of even feet and lines. But it would not do. Her genius revolted, and again and again carried her over into cadence in spite of herself. Here is a poem, part metre, part cadence:

VI

Peril as a possession
'Tis good to bear,
Danger disintegrates satiety;
There's Basis there
Begets an awe,
That searches Human Nature's creases
As clean as Fire.

The first two lines are perfect metre, the third is cadence, the fourth and fifth again are metre, while cadence returns in the sixth and seventh.

A knowledge of the principles of unitary verse (that is, verse based upon a unit of time instead of a unit of accent) would have liberated Emily Dickinson from the bonds against which she chafed. But she was of too unanalytical a nature to find this for herself, consciously; that she found it subconsciously this poem proves:

XXVI

Victory comes late,
And is held low to freezing lips

Too rapt with frost
To take it.
How sweet it would have tasted,
Just a drop!
Was God so economical?
His table's spread too high for us
Unless we dine on tip-toe.
Crumbs fit such little mouths,
Cherries suit robins;
The eagle's golden breakfast
Strangles them.
God keeps his oath to sparrows,
Who of little love
Know how to starve!

There is one other way in which Emily Dickinson was a precursor of the Imagists. She, first of all in English I believe, made use of what I have called elsewhere the 'unrelated' method. That is, the describing of a thing by its appearance only, without regard to its entity in any other way. Even to-day, the Imagists are, so far as I know, the only poets to employ this device. Mr. Fletcher constantly uses it in his 'Symphonies,' but they are too long to quote. This little poem, however, will serve as an example of the *genre*:

THE SKATERS

TO A. D. R.

Black swallows swooping or gliding
In a flurry of entangled loops and curves;

The skaters skim over the frozen river.
And the grinding click of their skates as they impinge
      upon the surface,
Is like the brushing together of thin wing-tips of silver.

Now hear Emily Dickinson on a humming-bird:

THE HUMMING–BIRD

A route of evanescence
With a revolving wheel;
A resonance of emerald;
A rush of cochineal;
And every blossom on the bush
Adjusts its tumbled head, —
The mail from Tunis, probably,
An easy morning's ride.

'She was not daily-bread,' says her niece, 'she was star-dust.' Do we eat stars more readily than we did, then? I think we do, and if so, it is she who has taught us to appreciate them.

CONTEMPORARIES

TWO GENERATIONS IN AMERICAN POETRY

SOME fifty years ago, more or less, a handful of unrelated men and women took to being born up and
down these United States. What impulse was responsible for them, what submerged law of change
and contradiction settled upon them as its tools,
it is a little hard to say — at least, to say in any
sort of reasonable compass. They appear to have
been sporadic efforts of some force or other, oper-
ating over a period of nearly fifteen years; but so
disconnected were they, geographically, socially,
and atavistically, that one thing is certain: however they may have derived from a central urge,
they did not derive in the least from one another.
This little handful of disconnected souls, all un-
obtrusively born into that America which sighed
with Richard Watson Gilder, wept with Ella
Wheeler Wilcox, permitted itself to dance deli-
cately with Celia Thaxter, and occasionally to
blow a graceful blast on the beribboned trumpet
of Louise Imogen Guiney, was destined to startle
its progenitors. This was a world of sweet appreciation, a devotee of caged warblers, which
species of gentle music-makers solaced it monthly

from the pages of the 'Century' or the 'Atlantic
Monthly.' How pleasant to turn away for a moment from the rattle of drays and horse-cars and
listen to a woodland strain repeated in a familiar
and well-loved cadence! That these robins of ours
were doing their best to imitate the notes of
English blackbirds and nightingales only made
their efforts the more precious, and, to be sure,
their imitations were done with a modesty worthy
of all admiration. They knew their place in the
world's harmony and saw to it that they did not
overstep it. This was expected and loyally ad-
hered to. What of America had time for these not
too exciting titivations of the emotions harkened
and was pleased; the busy rest of the populace
heeded not at all and missed very little.

Now, how it was that a handful of young persons, growing up in the seventies and eighties (for
the widely spaced arrivals lasted so long), found
themselves, one and all, so out of sympathy with
the chaste and saccharine music wandering
through the ambient air of current periodicals, is
one of the wonders of psychological phenomena.
It is a fact, nevertheless, that with no one to talk
to or compare notes with, each as separate as conditions could well make him, one and all they revolted against the taste of their acquaintances,
and launched, the whole flotilla of them, out into

the turbulent sea of experiment and personal expression.

Upheavals make for art, as is well known. The débâcle of the Franco-Prussian war gave France the galaxy of poets and musicians which made the last two decades of the nineteenth century so rich a period in her annals. But here, in America, there had been no war sufficiently recent to cause an effect of leaf-turning. The Civil War was too long gone by. No, the change in poetry seems to have sprung from something far more prosaic. From the great tide of commerce and manufacture, indeed. Prosperity is the mother of art, no matter how odd such an idea may seem. Look at the Elizabethan age in England. It followed immediately upon an expansion of the world's markets, did it not? But this expansion was all bound up with the romance of daring adventure and exploration. Quite so, and was not ours? A continent crossed and settled at infinite peril; rivers run into clacking factories; electricity caught and chained to wires, forcing the very air to obedient echo — are not such things as these romantic and adventurous? Whether people had the wit to see them in this light or not, the little devils who rule the psychological currents which man ignores and invariably obeys found them so. Nemesis is extraordinarily ironical. While the men of the race were making fortunes, and the women were going to concerts and puzzling their heads over a Browning whom, having invented themselves, they could not in the least understand, so different was he from dear Mr. Gilder — while all this was going on, in New England, the Middle West, in Pennsylvania and Arkansas, by one, and one, and one, like beads before they are strung upon a string, the makers of this poetic renaissance of ours were obscurely working all toward one end and that as various as the strands in a piece of rope.

Who the pioneers of this movement were, I am not going to say. They are perfectly well known to every one interested in present-day literature. Besides, we are still too near to them to render absolute statement possible. Were a suffrage taken, some names would appear in all lists, others would differ. Time alone can make the actual personnel of the movement secure. My intention here is to analyse a movement, not criticize individual talents. When I mention such, I do so as illustration merely.

With all their diversity, there was a central aim which bound the group together. Conscious with some, unconscious with others, their aim was to voice America. Now you cannot voice one country in the accents of another. Therefore the immediate object of these poets was to drop the perpetual imitation of England. It is interesting, if painful, to realize what a desperately hard time these young poets had. When they could get themselves printed, which was seldom, they were either completely ignored or furiously lampooned. And still they were alone, none knew the others; but they were a courageous little band, and on they went, writing, and putting their poems in their writing-table drawers.

Suddenly, explosively, the movement came to a head in 1912 and the years immediately succeeding. In October, 1912, Harriet Monroe brought out her magazine 'Poetry,' but, splendid work though that magazine has done, I cannot subscribe to its often expressed opinion that it is largely responsible for the recognition the group began to achieve. Instead I should say that it was another manifestation of the fulminating spirit which produced the poets themselves. Every one of these poets had been writing for years, some of them for many years, others were already the authors of neglected volumes, before 'Poetry' arrived on the scene. It seems to me rather that the ferment had reached a point when it was bound to burst. For burst it did and bore down on the American consciousness with an indomitable violence not to be resisted. Horrified professors shuddered and took to umbrellas and arctics, newspaper fulminators

tried all the weapons in their armories from snubs
to guffaws. It was no use; what must come, comes.
The caged warblers were swept out of court. The
people who hated the new poetry were forced back
on the classical old which antedated the warbler
era. And that alone was a good thing.

But this movement which we speak of so glibly,
do we really know what it was? Let us observe it a
little. In the first place, it was an effort to free the
individual from the expression of the herd; in the
second, it had for its object the breaking down
of mere temperamental barriers. This looks like
paradox, but it is not. The poetry of the two preceding decades had been almost entirely concerned
with recording personal emotions, but recording
them in a perfectly stereotyped way. The new
poetry found that emotions were not confined to
the conjugation of the verb to love, and whether it
said 'I love' or 'Behold the earth and all that is
thereon,' if it followed its natural inclination, it
would say it quite differently from the way its
fathers had said it. The truth is that this new
poetry, whether written by men or women, was in
essence masculine, virile, very much alive. Where
the nineties had warbled, it was prone to shout.
When it concerned itself with love, its speech was
natural and unrestrained; when not concerned
with love, it found interests as manifold as the

humanity crowding on its eyes from every street corner. It had so much to say that it simply could not say it, and so huge a country to speak for that no one poet could do more than present a little by-lane of it. It took the whole handful of poets which made up the group to give any adequate expression of the movement or the age which produced it; but, taking the work by and large, book after book, here was a volume of energy, a canvas so wide and sparkling, that something very like the dazzling tapestry of American life, thought, and activities was obtained.

As the poets were, so was their work. One gave simple facts; another approached the central truth obliquely; a third abandoned America as far as direct allusion went, and presented it the more clearly in reactions on distant countries and periods viewed through American eyes. For instance, take Frost and Sandburg and juxtapose them with 'H. D.' Not one of these three could have sprung from any country but America, and yet where Frost and Sandburg portray their special country-sides, town and open, 'H. D.' occupies herself with an ancient loveliness alive again through the eager vision of a young race to which nothing is stale. Wherever posterity may place the group in the rôle of American poets, one thing it cannot deny them: the endeavour after a major utterance.

They may have failed; they dared the stars. They hitched their wagons to the tails of comets. There was nothing the matter with their aim; success is another thing, and not for us to gauge.

The world learnt to like them pretty well, although they were not very much understood. It is not the way of our modern world to accord greatness its due, even when it slyly supposes that it may exist. The very feeble educations which are all most of us can boast tend to caution rather than to acclaim. It is safer to doubt, for then the odds are with you. No, the world was interested, but took refuge in the old cry: 'These men are precursors, we await the great poet for whom they are clearing the way.' And what happened? Rather a curious thing. At first the pioneers rolled up their tallies of disciples. Incipient 'Spoon Rivers' rippled on every side; bits of here, there, and everywhere à la Frost appeared; red-blooded followers travestied Sandburg's least successful pictures, stupidly unaware that it was his tenderness and insight which made him the man he was; the Imagists almost despaired of ever freeing themselves from the milk-and-water imitations with which young hopefuls flooded the non-paying magazines. Still the great poet who was to go all of them one better did not make his appearance. Instead came a *volte-face*. Reaction, by Jove! Or so it appeared. Reaction after ten years! But things move swiftly nowadays.

The bewildered elders rubbed their eyes. Had all their work been in vain? By no means, for the reaction owed more to them than it has ever been willing to acknowledge. Without them, the younger poets could not have existed. Now, constant reaction is a law of art. When one impulse is exhausted, the artistic undercurrents turn to another. Finding it impossible to outdistance the pioneers on their own ground, the next generation veered off at a tangent and sought other grounds of its own. But a reaction, to be effective, must produce poets of something like the calibre of the poets reacted from. Without attempting to answer this question one way or the other, we can, at least, peer a little more closely at the type of poetry coming on the stage to-day.

The younger group appears to be composed of two entirely distinct companies. Unlike the pioneers, who had among them the tie of a concerted effort, these two sections are completely at variance with one another. To name them: one calls itself the Secessionists; the other we may christen, for purposes of differentiation, the Lyrists. It is not a very good name, for all poets write lyrics, but as these poets write practically nothing else, it will serve. Of these two groups, the lyrists are unquestionably doing the better work. They proclaim no tenets, but confine themselves to writing poetry, and doing it uncommonly well. Their expertness is really amazing. They have profited by the larger movement in finding an audience readymade to their hands, a number of magazines eager to welcome them, and a considerable body of critical writing bearing on the poetical problems of the moment — aids to achievement which the older group entirely lacked. Through the practice of the elders, the younger group has learnt to slough off the worst faults of the nineties, and, in the matter of versification, there is scarcely a fault to be found with their work. I refer, of course, to that of the leaders. The strange thing here, however, the crux of the reactionary situation, is its aim. For where the older generation aimed at a major expression, these younger poets are directly forcing themselves to adhere to a minor one. The terms major and minor in poetry have nothing to do with good and bad; a minor poet is often meticulously careful and exceedingly fine. Major and minor refer to outlook, and it is a fact that this younger group deliberately seeks the narrow, personal note. It is a symptom, I suppose, a weariness of far horizons, a breath-taking before a final leap.

Where emotion is the chief stock in trade, we should not expect a high degree of intellectual content, yet in one member of the group we find it. Elinor Wylie, who, unlike Edna St. Vincent Millay, that delightfully clever exponent of the perennial theme of love, is one of the most intellectual and well equipped of American poets. These two are the acknowledged chiefs of the company. For, while the older movement was innately masculine, the new one is all feminine. It is, indeed, a feminine movement, and remains such even in the work of its men.

The Secessionists are quite apart. Their object is science rather than art; or perhaps it is fairer to say that to them art is akin to mathematics. They are much intrigued by structure, in a sense quite other than that in which it is usually employed in poetry. They have a host of theories, and are most interesting when stating them, but the doubt arises whether a movement which concerns itself more with statements about poetry than with the making of poetry itself is ever going to produce works of art of a quality to justify the space taken up by pronunciamentos.

The outcome of all this is somewhat hazy. It is a fact that, side by side with the youths, the elders are still writing. Whether the younger group will sweep aside the older, it is too soon to see. That the far easier poetry of the lyrists will be, and is, immensely popular, is only natural. The question is, how long can it maintain itself in the face of its wilfully restricted limits? Whether the future will bring a period of silence preceding another vigorous dash forward, or whether the present feminine mood will lead directly into the next advance, who shall say? Not I, at any rate. Both possibilities are in order, and for the present I think we may be satisfied. The time has been short, and considerable has been done in a variety of ways by the two generations at the moment writing. As Whitman said, here is 'a lapful of seed, and this is a fine country.'

WEARY VERSE

'Georgian Poetry, 1918–1919.' Edited by E. M. New York: G. P. Putnam's Sons.

IT is a profound labour to read this book. Not because, let me hastily say, there is nothing good in it, but because it is all so dreadfully tired.

Is this the exhaustion of the war, or is it the debility of an old habit of mind deprived of the stimulus of a new inspiration? It is an interesting question, for the fatigue is undeniable. Here are nineteen poets, in the heyday of their creating years, and scarcely one of them seems to have energy enough to see personally or forge a manner out of his own, natural speech. They are all respectable poets, each knows his trade and can turn out good enough verse on an old model, but how strangely one man's contribution dovetails into the next man's! This is happily not true of all, but it is true of the majority. Try it — for instance, who wrote this

> But this shall be the end of my delight:
> That you, my lovely one, shall stoop and see
> Your image in the mirrored beauty there.

And did the same man write this?

> And Cleopatra's eyes, that hour they shone
> The brighter for a pearl she drank to prove

How poor it was compared to her rich love:
But when I look on thee, love, thou dost give
Substance to those fine ghosts, and make them live.

Is this he again, or another?

Thy hand my hand,
Thine eyes my eyes,
All of thee
Caught and confused with me:
My hand thy hand,
My eyes thine eyes,
All of me
Sunken and discovered anew in thee.

And who is responsible for this?

Dear Love, whose strength no pedantry can stir
Whether in thine iron enemies,
Or in thine own strayed follower
Bemused with subtleties and sophistries,
Now dost thou rule the garden...

If the reader will play fairly and guess a bit, I
think he will find himself sufficiently bewildered.
The answer to the riddle is purely arbitrary. The
book says that Francis Brett Young is the author
of the first quotation and the other names, in order,
read: W. H. Davies, John Freeman, and Edward
Shanks. But, for all we can see to the contrary,
the names might be jumbled about in any order
without causing the slightest confusion in style or
attitude.

The reason is quite plain, Mr. Young, Mr. Davies, Mr. Freeman, Mr. Shanks are merely taking the place of our old friends Brown, Jones, and Robinson, or, to telescope the whole after the manner of a composite photograph, we might name them collectively John Doe. In other words, these gentlemen are not writing at all, it is their poetic ancestors who are writing, they have made themselves ouija boards for the recrudescence of a dead song.

There are notable exceptions to this, I am glad to say, and I shall come to them later, but on the whole, the book seems pale and spectre-like, haunted by the ghosts of England's vanished bards.

There is really no excuse for this, for even if these English poets choose to ignore the fresh vigour of American poetry, they have Masefield in England, and Ralph Hodgson, and Aldington, and Sassoon. It is stuff and nonsense to try and raise such echoes into the dignity of a poetic creed as Mr. Squire and Mr. Shanks are constantly trying to do. All literature is against them; good poets are not echoes, and never were, and that is the long and the short of it. I am told that Mr. T. S. Eliot is having a great influence in England and, although I am not a complete admirer of Mr. Eliot's style, I can well believe that he is needed in

a country where Mr. Young stalks abroad melli-
fluously bemoaning the duress of poethood in such
a new and striking phrase as: 'Whither, O my
sweet mistress, must I follow thee?' His own
words, farther on in the same poem, are more than
portrait; they are prophecy: 'The pillared halls of
sleep echoed my ghostly tread,'

He is a wonder, this Mr. Young, I can hardly
tear myself away from him. What a memory he
has, to be sure. Where have we read:

> With all the joy of Spring
> And morning in her eyes?

It is foolish to ask where; it would be much more
sensible to put it 'where not.' Certainly Mr.
Young challenges the spectres right smartly. He
speaks of 'snow upon the blast' of the 'livery of
death'; his moon is quite comfortably 'hornéd,'
with the accent all nicely printed over the last syllable. But let us give him his due, his cacophony
is original. Read this aloud:

> The frozen fallows glow, the black trees shaken
> In a clear flood of sunlight vibrating awaken.

But we must not leave Mr. Young alone in a
glorious isolation; that would be to do him too
much honour, for does not Mr. Davies speak of
'Yon full moon,' and Mr. Abercrombie com-
placently watch while 'The sun drew off at last his

piercing fires'; even Mr. Gibson, who is usually above such diction, permits himself to call the sea 'the changeless deep.'

One could go on poking fun forever—there is matter for it — but the thing is not funny; on the contrary, it is desperately sad. They want to be poets so much, these young men. They know they have something to say, they feel it doubtless, but they are like men uttering words in a dream; in the cold light of day, it comes perilously near nonsense, because it is nonsense to repeat by rote a thing which does not express one's thoughts. There is atrophy here; this stale stuff is not merely stale, it is pathological. We know what these young men want to say; the strong spirits among them have told us: they want to say how deeply they love England, how much the English countryside (the most beautiful countryside in the world) means to them; they detest war, and long for the past which cannot come back, and they hope fiercely for a future which, if they can, they will see to it shall be better. But the power to set down all this has been weakened by strain. They have not the energy to see personally, or speak with their own voices. The will to do so is strong; the nervous strength necessary for the task (and it requires much) is lacking.

The English countryside is here, but in all the

old tones and colours. Surely never book was so
swayed over by the branches of trees. Nightingales and thrushes abound, but seldom does the
poet get them alive on the page; he loves them, but
he slays them, and more's the pity.

This is not always true. Mr. Drinkwater's
'Chorus from "Lincoln"' is very England, although not quite so fine as his 'In Lady Street,'
which is not in this volume, and so is Mr. de la
Mare's 'Sunken Garden,' and Mr. Monro's 'Dog'
is fully successful. Even Mr. Davies gets himself
sometimes, since he can write:

Blink with blind bats' wings, and heaven's bright face
Twitch with the stars that shine in thousands there.

Mr. Davies tries to be himself, and it is unfortunate that we often wish he would not. When he de-
scribes a lark as 'raving' above the clouds, we feel
that his vocabulary is unwarrantably scanty, and
it is nonsense to speak of the 'merry sound of
moths' bumping on a ceiling. 'Merry' — watch-
ing the tortured struggles of the poor things to get
out — merry! He tells us that he is the 'dumb
slave' of a lady who brings 'great bursts' of music
out of a harpsichord; 'deaf' I think should be the
word, for I doubt if even a Liszt could force that
frail and delicate instrument to 'great bursts.'
Or, perish the thought, was the lady really playing

a piano, and did Mr. Davies merely think 'harpsi-chord' more poetical?

Yes, they do try, but often only to make a mess of it. When the nightingale does not sing, Mr. Nichols observes, 'Nor has the moon yet touched the brown bird's throat,' which is mighty fine writing of a kind usually found in 'Parlour Albums' and 'Gems from the Poets for Every Day in the Year.' Mr. Nichols has been reading the diction-ary, his boughs are 'labyrinthine,' the blossom of a lime tree is a 'hispid star of citron bloom,' and 'sigils' are burned into his heart and face. A sort of passion for the archaic seems to have got hold of him, we have 'flittest, profferest, blowest, renew-est,' all in four lines. Most of these poets love 'thees' and 'thous,' that horrible second person which everyday speech has happily got rid of. But Mr. Nichols is a good poet, only he does not hold himself up. To speak of the trunk of a tree as 'splitting into massy limbs' is excellent, but he spoils it by having the branches 'bowered in foliage,' and yet the man is often full of insight. Of a squirrel, he can say: 'He scrambled round on little scratchy hands,' and what could be finer than the 'peaked and gleaming face' of the dying man in 'The Sprig of Lime.' That whole poem touches a very high mark, and sets Mr. Nichols quite apart from the John Does.

As one glances through the four volumes of
'Georgian Poetry,' one cannot help wondering on
what principle they are edited. Scarcely on that
of presenting all the best poetry of the moment, it
would seem, since Richard Aldington, F. S. Flint,
the Sitwells, and Anna Wickham have never been
included. Mr. James Stephens, who had been in
from the beginning, has vanished, which is a great
loss; and Mr. Hodgson, who appeared in the second
and third issues, has also gone. It is understand-
able why Mr. Chesterton, as belonging to an older
group, has left, but Mr. Masefield, by all the laws
of literary relationship, should surely have remained. Is the editor, Mr. Marsh, sole arbiter,
and if so, why? When former contributors disappear, do they remove themselves, or are they
assisted to depart? And again, in either case, why?

It is horrible to reflect on the power of an editor.
Poets, at the mercy of editorial selection, may well
tremble, reflecting on the fate of the Dutch painter
Vermeer, who vanished for nearly three hundred
years from the knowledge of men because a contemporary writer with whom he was so ill-advised
as to quarrel omitted him from a list of painters
which was destined to become the textbook of
future generations.

Mr. Marsh edits with well-defined prejudices,
evidently, but, on the whole, he has accomplished

much, for he has brought the authors of his anthologies a wide publicity. For those who go out,
others come in. Mr. Graves, and Mr. Sassoon,
who, with Mr. Squire, appeared first in the
1916–17 anthology, are the chiefs of the new-
comers. The most powerful poem in the book is
Mr. Sassoon's 'Repression of War Experience.'
The war made Mr. Sassoon a poet. He needed to
be torn and shaken by a great emotion; he has
found this emotion in his detestation of war.
Nothing stronger than these poems, which are the
outgrowth of his suffering, has been written in
England since the war 'stopped our clocks.' It
would be hard to make a selection of them, and
really it does not matter; one side of a heart is a
good deal like the other side provided it be a real
flesh and blood heart. In this case it is, and wherever you take it, you get the same sensation. There
is no rhetoric here, we are not treated to erudite
expressions nor literary artifices, and for that reason these poems, and 'Repression' especially,
come perilously near to being great. I say 'perilously,' for what is Mr. Sassoon going to do now?
When was 'Everyone Sang' written? Perhaps
that points a new departure.

Mr. Sassoon and Mr. Graves feel so much that
they can afford to joke about it. Mr. Sassoon's
joking is a shade more bitter, more ironical. For

instance, 'What Does It Matter?' is a trifle harder and heavier than Mr. Graves's 'It's a Queer Time,' which unfortunately is not in this volume. Neither is 'I Wonder What It Feels Like to be Drowned.' But one cannot have all a man's collected works in an anthology, and we have got that fine thing, 'A Frosty Night,' and the possibly even finer 'The Cupboard.' Mr. Graves is that delightful being among poets, a *faux naïf.* He runs his ballad forms hard but so far they do not fade upon the palate.

Miss Shove is a notable addition to this year's anthology. She has originality and a saving sense of the grotesque and macabre. 'The New Ghost' is excellent.

Of the original contributors, Mr. Abercrombie's poetry is always a strange mixture of the quick and the dead. He builds live tales on a pattern of rusty pins. The result is according as one feels about the vexed question of subject and treatment. I confess that I find Mr. Abercrombie worthy of respect, but dull.

Mr. Davies has ardent admirers, and I am quite aware that my making him sit as part portrait for the highly estimable John Doe will probably cause much offence. If only Mr. Davies would always write poems like 'A Child's Pet,' would always keep to such natural speech as that in the first

four lines of 'England,' I would readily subtract
him from the sum total of my composite hero.
But Mr. Davies has read books, and they have remained in his mind alien and undigested. Therefore he must give his quota to John Doe, and I
regretfully beg his pardon.

Mr. de la Mare is scarcely at his best in this
volume, although 'The Sunken Garden' is very
charming. But I cannot forgive him his last line
with the false rhyme. False rhyming is often a
most happy device, but scarcely here, where there
have been no other such rhymes in the poem, and
for the last line — particularly when he had a perfect rhyme in his adjective! Clearly the sound did
not trouble Mr. de la Mare's ear, but it teases
mine horribly.

Mr. Drinkwater is a poet who must be read in a
certain mood. His poems do not yield all their
fragrance if they are hastily approached or vio-
lently attempted. They grow on the reader as of
something becoming conscious. They seem extraordinarily simple, by every preconceived canon
they should be dull, and behold, they are neither
the one nor the other. The best of them, that is,
and two of the best are here: 'Moonlit Apples' and
'Habitation,' while 'Chorus from "Lincoln,"' the
first half especially, is nearly as good. What is
Mr. Drinkwater's charm? how does he escape the

sensation of écho, considering that he chooses to write in a traditional mode? To analyse it with any care would take up too much space here; in brief, I think it lies in his utter abandonment to his poem, in his complete sincerity in regard to it, in his straightforward, unselfconscious love of what he is writing about. He is a quiet poet, he keeps his drama for his plays, but his dramatic sense has taught him the secret of creating atmosphere. 'Moonlit Apples' is beautifully moony. But this simplicity and this atmosphere are not accidental; they are built up with delicate touch after touch throughout the poem. One could wish that 'In Lady Street' had been included and 'Southampton Bells' left out, but, on the whole, his selection is one of the best in the book.

Mr. Gibson's 'Cakewalk' is a good poem, and so is the first stanza of 'Parrots'; the latter is a complete poem by itself; the second stanza adds nothing, it even detracts appreciably. Why must Mr. Gibson bring in his heart? the Parrots did so well without it.

Mr. Lawrence's 'Seven Seals' is in his most mystical and passionate vein. The poem is serious and exalted, but it is a pity that it should be his only contribution; it would stand better were it companioned. As a poet, Mr. Lawrence is rising in stature year by year; his last volume, 'Bay,' is the best book of poetry, pure poetry, that he has written, although it does not reach the startling human poignance of 'Look! We Have Come Through.' It is unfair to Mr. Lawrence to be represented by one poem; the editor should take heed and give us more of him in future.

Mr. Monro improves steadily. I have already mentioned his beautiful and exceedingly satisfactory 'Dog.' I wish I had space to quote it. It is not only good poetry, but good dog. Mr. Monro's work is gaining in muscle. Beauty it has often had, but now there is a firm structure under the beauty — see, for instance, 'Man Carrying Bail.' 'The Nightingale Near the House' was a bold challenge to Fate, but Mr. Monro has come through fairly successfully. His nightingale lives and sings, and not too reminiscently, which is much for a modern nightingale to do.

For the newer men, Mr. Squire is a clever fellow. His criticisms, even if one disagree with them, are always interesting. His poetry is clever too, and that is not so useful an attribute in poetry. But he has done some good things. 'August Moon,' with its marvellous description of moonlight on water, is not here (really we must quarrel with the editor for leaving it out) but another of his best things, the 'Sonnet,' is. Few modern sonnets are as good as this; the last two lines are magnificent. 'Rivers' begins well, with an original and fluctuating rhythm which gives the lapsing and flowing of a river to a remarkable degree, and the slight change between the first and second stanza is well conceived. But then he becomes tangled in his own creation, the metre stiffens into a convention, becomes hard, unimaginative, and cold, and the poem loses itself in a long and rather stupid catalogue.

Mr. Turner, who appears for the second time, has a nice little quality — he has his own turns, and a very pleasant whimsical touch:

> The thronged, massed, crowded multitude of leaves
> Hung like dumb tongues that loll and gasp for air

gives an effect we have all seen, most vividly. 'Tinkling like polished tin' has the thin sharpness of tone of a small stream, and 'old wives cried their wares, like queer day owls' is very nice. 'Silence' is a good poem, but the best of those here is 'Talking With Soldiers,' with its refrain 'the mind of the people is like mud,' and then the dreaming iridescence.

Of the remaining poets — but why catalogue the virtues or record the faults of John Doe?

STOCK–TAKING, AND A PARTICULAR INSTANCE

'Breakers and Granite.' By John Gould Fletcher. New York: The Macmillan Company. 1921.

How does a writer catch the public ear? That is a question so subtle as to take much pondering. And when we substitute 'poet' for 'writer,' the matter becomes even more confused. Poetry is never written for the general reader, as novels often are, because great masses of people have not, and can never have, the slightest comprehension of what poetry is. Poetry is a special way of observing life, just as love is a special way of feeling, but love is a universal emotion (in its basic form, at least), while poetry, following some obscure design, can only be experienced by a comparatively restricted section of any community.

Those poems which have enjoyed a real popularity in their day, such as Walter Scott's, and Byron's, in the early nineteenth century; or Alfred Noyes's for a brief couple of years in this country; or Lisshauer's 'Hymn of Hate' in Germany at the beginning of the war, are usually found to have made their appeal because of some quality quite apart from the poetry in them.

Out of the very small number of people who love poetry because it is poetic, how shall the poet find the even smaller number who are going to like his particular brand? Advertising, as the publishers understand it, is almost useless. When a man is known, his admirers like to be told that a new book of his is available, but the poet gains his first readers by some process of appeal so delicate and hidden as to defy research. Advertising causes notoriety, but I doubt very much whether it makes readers; in some cases it even has the opposite effect. The poet and his readers converge together in accordance with some strange psychic law, and the quality of the reading public can be very accurately gauged by the poets they encourage. Suppose we imagine two poets equally able in their art, that one with the largest following will be a gauge to the temper of the public.

I have been noting the course of poetry for many years, and I am convinced that in this country (and more so here than in any other, I believe) even the genuine poetry-readers have but a slight love and knowledge of the poetry in a poem; the so-called 'human appeal,' the story element, is the delighting thing. We are not, in America, very luxuriant thinkers; we are considerably afraid of exuberance of imagination; it not only does not attract, it causes a definite movement of recoil.

Those poets addicted to richness of colouring and wealth of imagery suffer from the very glorious-ness of their imaginations. We can stand a great deal of banality or baldness of poetic feeling if only the subject be firmly enough planted on the ground; but we are thrown into a convulsion of distaste if the poet, seeing a lovely earth and tell-ing us how he sees it, forget to reduce this seeing to the mere background of a love-tale, or a death-tale, or something equally familiar and reassuring. All of which is merely to repeat the old truism that the American public is inexperienced.

The present poetic revival has proved one thing, however, it has proved that a great many of the younger generation are seeing things which their ancestors never saw. It has proved that the American is a highly original animal if he can ever work himself up to throw off the standardized thinking imposed upon him by herd education; if he can once squash the fatal ideal to be just like everybody else. Youth tells us, with gusto, that 'you can say anything now,' and that is good so far as it goes. Dear dead Queen Victoria was use-ful, no doubt, but I am not sorry that her shadow is lifting from us. Still an indiscriminate playing at skittles with reticencies is not only a rather childish pastime, it becomes a wearying conven-tion, which brings me to another point. Are we not, perhaps, moulding a new set of conventions quite as bitter to wear as those we are trying to throw off? Who makes the audience for these inexpert and jejune revelations? The same public which has enjoyed such things since the days of Adam, no doubt, and no more interested in poetry than it ever has been.

It is time that somebody called to the poets and the audiences to 'watch their step.' It is time that the poets and the audiences grew up. It is high time that the young poets took themselves seriously and learnt something about their art so that they may practise it with the utmost freedom and originality, and without making absurd blunders such as believing indecency to be a new thing in the world. It is high time, too, that audiences should love poetry enough to gain some measure of criticism in regard to it, in order that they may at least learn the false from the true. To consider D. H. Lawrence as immoral is certainly to misunderstand his terrible and pathetic questioning; to give a serious thought to Dadaism is to be simply a dupe.

I do not see one tithe of the originality and vigour in the young English poets that I do in ours. But they do know a lot more about their job than the majority of those here. With their knowledge and our power, what might we not do! Hostile audi-

ences would be made to sit up and their glaives of
sarcasm would turn upon themselves; over-kind
audiences would cease to obscure the landscape
with scented vapourings; women's clubs would
cease to fuddle their brains over the pronounce-
ments of half-baked lecturers; and Mr. Fletcher's
poetry would, I think, receive a measure of its
just due.

I am supposed to be reviewing 'Breakers and
Granite,' his last book, and my opening question
was prompted by the very obvious fact that Mr.
Fletcher has, as yet, failed in great measure to
find his special audience. What is the reason?
Here is a man of so true an originality that no
prototype can be found for him in the past. A
poet with a marvellous vision for the beauty
which is in the world, and with an abundant power
to express that vision, and yet he is far less popular than poets greatly his inferiors. His first two
books, 'Irradiations' and 'Goblins and Pagodas,'
were, quite evidently, not understood. The fear
of exuberance, of which I have spoken, operated
powerfully against them. They took people's
breath away. It was sad and unjust; it was the
reaction of an unwise public. His next book, 'The
Tree of Life,' being a volume of love-songs, was
much more successful. Now, with this volume,
'Breakers and Granite.' Mr. Fletcher is on new

ground. He has given us a vast and cloudy epic of America which, at this particular time, is most significant.

There seem to be two marked trends in American poetry at the moment. In one of them locality is predominant, and locality seen from the point of view of the novelist even if presented in the manner of the poet. In this poetry, persons and places together make up a series of events. Mr. Masters, with the 'Spoon River Anthology' and 'Domesday Book,' stands for the extreme of the type, but Mr. Frost and Mr. Robinson. in their more poetic ways, usually work in the same genre. With Mr. Sandburg, the human element dominates the element of event, but he, too, strives to express a general life rather than a particular; his desire is to express men, rather than the particular man, and his vision is, only less than Mr. Masters', bound by a rather narrow horizon. Mr. Robinson's depth comes from his escape from the ticking of the parlour clock back into a wider time, but, even with this escape, he remains rooted in fact. This statement, however, must be taken, not as a criticism, but as an analysis. By it we can reach an understanding of the other trend in which the poet speaks as himself, and, being himself, not as general man, but man of a highly specialized sort.

This personal poetry uses its environment

merely as atmosphere; the emphasis is laid on the writer's reactions to it and its effect upon his emotions. This type of poetry has managed to free itself from the past more completely than has the other, which has been both an advantage and a disadvantage. Where the poet has been a true artist, an earnest experimenter, the result has been good; where he has been merely concerned in outdoing others in queerness he has failed and brought derision upon the talented and the untalented alike. The imitators of the first group are merely dull; the imitators of the second are a weariness to the flesh. But we must not let this weariness blind us to the fact that the pioneers of what we call the 'new poetry' sprang from this section; though they, with a vigour which the hangers-on cannot imitate, have gone on developing. While a host of young people were copying (though at a great distance) Mr. Fletcher's 'Irradiations,' Mr. Fletcher himself was growing, changing, opening his mind to deeper influences. He was always extraordinarily original, but his early work was almost entirely concerned with fugitive impressions, and mostly with impressions of scenes.

In my 'Tendencies in Modern American Poetry,' I pointed out that when Mr. Fletcher had learnt to feel humanity as he did nature, he would become one of the most important of living poets.

'The Tree of Life' showed his interest turning that way. In 'Breakers and Granite' we see a farther advance along the road; this time it is not love of a person which moves him, but love of a country. Through this book, he makes a certain connection with the two groups I have mentioned and yet remains individual and aloof from both.

Here is America, East, and West, and Middle. Mr. Fletcher sees his country with grandeur, with love, even with sorrow, with a mighty rejoicing. Poet, patriot, lover, Mr. Fletcher gives us America from all these angles. His attitude is inclusive and sweeping, not detailed. It is a synthesis of imaginative aspects, of broad and immensely beautiful effects. He grasps the significance of each section of the country, realizes whence its forces come, to what they are tending. What gazer on the skies at dawn from a New York apartment house can fail to recognize the truth of this description?

Ivory and gold, heart of light petrified, bold and immortally beautiful, lifts a tower like a full lily stalk with crammed pollen-coated petals, flame-calyx, fretted and carven, white phœnix that beats its wings in the light, shrill ecstasy of leaping lines poised in flight, partaker of joy in the skies, mate of the sun.

Again, New York is a

> White lily hammered out of steel,
> Upspraying, strangely beautiful.

These are scenes again, but they are more than scenes, for humanity is implied behind them. This awakened love of humanity pulses through the whole book and gives it a depth which 'Irradiations' and 'Goblins and Pagodas' never had. 'The Fuel Vendor,' one of the Arizona poems, is a beautiful thing. It is too long to quote in full, but this verse indicates its quality:

> My life is a stony plain,
> In which I gather twisted sticks;
> The heat and the strain
> Of hunger ever watching me,
> The rose-and-opal mystery
> Of the silence;
> And the peaks like great black altars of death
> Against the scarlet of the evening.

Mr. Fletcher's historical sense is merely his impression of humanity in the mass. The pathos of the Southern poems is that of one who has lived amid the suffering of the aftermath of the Civil War. 'The Old South,' 'The Changing South,' and 'Gettysburg' are excellent in conception and in execution, and in their strength of emotion beyond either. These poems link together to make a sort of prologue to 'Lincoln,' which becomes all the greater if we advance to it from them. I have said before, and I repeat, that I find Mr. Fletcher's 'Lincoln' surpassed by no other poem on the subject I have ever read.

'The Poem of the Mist' is the struggle and urge of America in the great fevers of birth and her three wars. 'The Great River' is more lyrical, as are also the 'Arizona Poems,' the best of which, I think, are 'The Windmills,' 'The Fuel Vendor,' and 'Rain in the Desert' with its beautiful last stanza. But, personally, I prefer 'Clipper-Ships' to anything in the volume. Five pages, and we have the essence of all the books on the subject, and all the meaning which the books do not give us. 'Beautiful as a tiered cloud, sky-sails set and shrouds twanging,' he starts the key at once. What could be better than this, in a tropic calm, or almost a calm: 'She ghosts along before an imperceptible breeze, the sails hanging limp in the cross-trees, and clashing against the masts. She is a proud white albatross skimming across the ocean, beautiful as a tiered cloud.' But the poem must be read; no quotations can give its flavour.

A warning, however: the book should not be read through at a sitting. There is too little drop in the emotion to admit of that with profit. If the poems are read each for itself and spaced, not too many at a time, the force of the whole book will be better felt.

What Mr. Fletcher has not is patent enough; he has no instinct for telling a story, he employs neither wit nor satire, he is dramatic only in the large. What he has are his own unique perceptions and impressions, great knowledge, love of colour, form, and significance, and understanding to interpret the forces behind the actions of men. Must he wait for death to bring him his audience, or will some moment of insight teach our public that here is a man so unlike anybody else as to be dangerous to ignore? The more knowledge a person has, the better will he understand this poetry. If it make demands upon its readers, it is at least abundantly able to satisfy them.

POETRY AND PROPAGANDA

'Smoke and Steel.' By Carl Sandburg. New York: Harcourt, Brace & Howe.

THIS little poetry renaissance of ours is getting along toward middle age. In other words, the poets who are chiefly responsible for it have each a number of volumes to their credit; are beginning, severally, to be masters of a manner, their own manner; are, in short, standing forth as persons of individual points of view and speech. Which is merely to say that they are passing out of the plastic, experimental stage, into the crystallizing and presumably permanent one. What they now are, they will probably remain. We must no more reckon them as promising; what they have done must be counted as achievement, even if, happily, an achievement by no means yet rounded out.

Professor Lowes, in a recent review of 'A Miscellany of American Poetry,' acknowledges that American poetry has a distinct colour of its own, that it is, in fact, forging for itself an original idiom. The very diversity of this idiom makes it but the more truly national. If any one will compare this 'Miscellany' with the latest 'Georgian Anthology,' the extraordinary unlikeness of the two books will be at once apparent. Starting-points for the American departure are not easy to find if we search more than superficially. Whom are they following, these eleven hard-writing, enthusiastic persons? No 'whom,' I believe, but a 'what.' I think they may most properly be defined as following 'the lay of the land.' It is the soil, and the winds and weather which pass over it, which have given them both vision and tongue.

In the first place, these are Northern poets braced against an unyielding climate; but this climate is not only unyielding, it is capricious, and requires a certain alertness of adaptation to cope with it at all. Professor Lowes bewails the absence of calm pellucid pools of verse, but why on earth should one expect calm pellucid pools with a thermometer forever playing leap-frog, winding the nervous system up and down a dozen times in a week? We may love the paintings of Fra Angelico, but who would expect to find his azure-and-pink-robed saints upon the canvases of our contemporaries? Sky-scraper architecture recalls the strange old ruins of Assyria and Egypt in its superb, brutal force. Look at these huge, marching blocks of masonry cutting the sky, treading down the little streets at their feet, do they at all resemble Saint-Martins-in-the-Fields, or the Houses of Parliament, or Saint Paul's? They are

less beautiful, as civilized man conceives beauty;
they are ruthless, because they represent the triumph of might. We may shudder at them as at
something splendid and barbaric, but we must admit their grandeur; and we shall admit it if we
imagine them for a moment as ruined, and if we
conceive of ourselves as tourists gazing at the tremendous, terrifying débris of a vanished world.
Being of them and not beyond them, we think of
them in other terms. We make them because we
need them, but we prefer a different speech of
architecture because we have been taught to prefer it.

All this is, if paradoxical, perfectly natural.
Professor Lowes prefers pellucid pools, he wants
another speech of poetry; but this is our speech,
we make it because we must, because it expresses
us. Personally I think it is a fine thing to have an
original speech, in architecture, in poetry, in anything whatsoever, provided it be real speech and
not an artificial jargon.

Another thing is, these poets are young and of
diverse races; even those of pure Anglo-Saxon
stock have been so mixed and ground about among
other peoples that they too are changed. Again,
they live in a broken world, they see darkly, they
hope highly, they make boisterously. They struggle under the eternal grief, urge, and vision of the

pioneer. What a huge, inchoate thing is this America of ours! The poets are like men hewing blocks of granite with pocket-knives. What use to ask them for nosegays of flowers, when all they have is a few flakes of rock. But pocket-knives may remove mountains if worked with the blind will of a fanatic. Call us blind fanatics, if you will; we believe that in time the rocks will yield us gardens. And here I think we have an allegory of Carl Sandburg, digging away at a hard stone, clearing a little flower-place here, blunting his knife there, keeping on because of something in him, and it is our grandsons who will know whether he has left them fruits or a desert of chipped pebbles.

Two men speak in Mr. Sandburg, a poet and a propagandist. His future will depend upon which finally dominates the other. Since a poet must speak by means of suggestion, and a propagandist succeeds by virtue of clear presentation, in so far as a propagandist is a poet, just in that ratio is he a failure where his propaganda is concerned. On the other hand, the poet who leaves the proper sphere of his art to preach, even by analogy, must examine the mote in his verse very carefully lest, perchance, it turn out a beam.

In my study of Mr. Sandburg in 'Tendencies in Modern American Poetry,' I pointed out this

danger of his practice. Then I had only one book
to go upon; now I have three, and the danger
seems to me to be looming larger with terrific
speed. It may be that Mr. Sandburg has determined to stuff all his theories into one book and let
it go at that. In which case there cannot be too
much objection, but I fear — oh, I fear.

Mr. Sandburg loves people, perhaps I should
say 'the people.' But I believe it is more than that.
I think he has a real love for human beings. But
evidently, from his books, his experience with
people is limited to a few types, and it is a pity
that these types should so often be the kind of
persons whom only the morbidly sensitive, un-
healthily developed, modern mind has ever
thought it necessary to single out for prominence
— prominence of an engulfing sort, that is. If we
admit that the degraded are degraded, there is not
much danger of losing our perspective; if we hug
them to our hearts and turn a cold shoulder to the
sober and successful of the world, then we are
running fast toward chaos, and our mental processes may fairly be considered a trifle askew. If
nature had deemed the unfit so important, she
would doubtless have heaped her favours upon
them instead of markedly reserving these tokens
for the fit. Setting the unfit on their feet is a good
deal like acting as pin-boy in a bowling-alley. It

is a pleasant pastime, if you like that sort of thing;
but as a life-work it seems abortive. Those pleasant individuals who advocate the stability of human nine-pins always remind me of the irate
reformer who besought his auditors to force the
repeal of 'this iniquitous law of supply and demand.'

In 'Cornhuskers,' Mr. Sandburg seemed content to let the back-alley folk stay in the back
alleys. He spoke to us of other things, of the great
wide prairies, for instance, and, in so speaking,
achieved a masterpiece. He gave his lyrical gift
far more space than he usually allows, and the result was some of the finest poems of the modern
movement. For Mr. Sandburg has a remarkable
originality. His outlook is his own, his speech
meets it, together the two make rarely beautiful
poetry, when Mr. Sandburg permits. Then con-
science pricks him, the 'people' rise and confront
him, gibbering like ghouls, he experiences an un-
easy sense of betrayal, and writes 'Galoots,' for
example. I think these things hurt Mr. Sandburg
as much as the things they represent hurt him. If
they did not hurt him they would not have become an obsession. Much morbid verse has been
written by tortured lovers, and we shall never
understand these particular poems of Mr. Sandburg's until we realize that he too is a tortured

lover, a lover of humanity in travail. It is seldom that the kind of exaggerated misery which Mr. Sandburg feels produces good poetry, and these poems are seldom successful. A few do justify themselves and I shall mention them later, but on the whole it is not in this mood that Mr. Sandburg does his best work.

I do not wish to imply that all the poems in this book are the results of the mood in question. That is far from the case, but the proportion of such poems is too great for the thorough satisfaction of a reader who is a profound admirer of Mr. Sandburg at his best — and, shall I add? his most lyrical. The book is divided into eight sections, of which only two, 'Mist Forms' and 'Haze,' are frankly lyrical, while another two, 'People Who Must' and 'Circle of Doors,' are as frankly the other thing which, for want of a better name, we may call 'the obsession.' But this obsession creeps into many poems in the sections 'Playthings of the Wind' and 'Passports'; even when 'it,' specifically, is not present, some crude and irrelevant turn of speech, the outgrowth of it, will crop up and ruin an otherwise noble thing. Colloquialisms, downright slang, have their place in poetry as in all literature. My contention here is not that Mr. Sandburg does not often use them with happy effect, but that, quite as often, he

drags them in where (to my ear, at least) they
should emphatically not be. A line like 'We'll get
you, you sbxyzch!' may be perfect realism, but it
hurts the reader, as does 'stenogs' and 'thinga-
majig.' The last appears in a poem in which it is
at least in place if we admit the poem itself,
'Manual System,' to a place anywhere; but
'stenogs' is smashed into a serious poem called
'Trinity Peace,' which is built round a highly
poetic thought. 'Stenographers' would not have
been out of order, because it is a mere description
of a calling, and in one stanza Mr. Sandburg is
enumerating people by their callings; to shorten
the word into 'stenogs' brings in an element of
cheapness which, in this instance, has no dramatic
value and so rivets the attention as to break the
force of the poem. One can skip such sheer propaganda as 'Alley Rats,' 'The Mayor of Gary,' and
'The Liars' if one wants to, but it is hard to have
something otherwise beautiful spoilt by a line or
a word which is hopelessly out of key.   It dis-
locates the mood of appreciation, and is, I believe,
the chief cause why the general reader does not
yet entirely recognize how fine and true a poet Mr.
Sandburg is.

Having registered my protest, which is the
disagreeable part of the critic's work, let me immediately admit that one of Mr. Sandburg's ex-

cellencies is that he sets down the life about him,
that very life of the people of which I have been
speaking. When he sees it as a poet, he makes it
poetically adequate; it is only when he sees it
obliquely as a biassed sentimentalist that he in-
jures it and himself. He has an inclusive vision,
something which gathers up the essences of life
and work and relates them to the pulsing fabric
which is the whole energy of human existence.
His 'Prairie' was not only a slice of Mother Earth;
it was Mother Earth cherishing her children. So,
in 'Smoke and Steel,' we have not a mere metal
being manufactured, not mere men toiling at their
work; we have man's impulse to spend himself in
creation, and the far ramifications of what that
creation means. We have the eye which sees the
beauty of the curves of smoke:

> Smoke of the fields in spring is one,
> Smoke of the leaves in autumn another.
> Smoke of a steel-mill roof or a battleship funnel,
> They all go up in a line with a smokestack,
> Or they twist... in the slow twist... of the wind.
>
> If the north wind comes they run to the south.
> If the west wind comes they run to the east.
> > By this sign
> > all smokes
> > know each other.
> Smoke of the fields in spring and leaves in autumn,

Smoke of the finished steel, chilled and blue,
By the oath of work they swear: 'I know you.'
        .   .   .   .

In the rolling mills and sheet mills,
In the harr and boom of the blast fires,
The smoke changes its shadow
And men change their shadow.

Nature and man are welded together for 'smoke and blood is the mix of steel.'

'Smoke and Steel' is worthy to stand beside 'Prairie.' There is an epic sweep to this side of Mr. Sandburg's work. Somehow it brings the reader into closer contact with his country; reading these poems gives me more of a patriotic emotion than ever 'The Star-Spangled Banner' has been able to do. This is America, and Mr. Sandburg loves her so much that suddenly we realize how much we love her too. What has become dulled by habit quickens under his really magical touch. Freight cars mean all the prosperity of the country; in the first stanza of 'Work Gangs,' they become a great chorus of men's hearts building a land to live in, to grow and make homes and happiness in. Because he can do this, Mr. Sandburg has a glorious responsibility set on his shoulders.

The seeing eye — Mr. Sandburg has it to a superlative degree, and, wedded to it, an imaginative utterance which owes nothing whatever to

literature or tradition. It is a fascinating and
baffling study, this of examining how Mr. Sandburg does it. The technique of this magic is so
unusual that no old knowledge applies. It is, more
than anything else, the sharp, surprising rightness
of his descriptions which gives Mr. Sandburg his
high position in the poetry of to-day. Here are a
few taken at random:

> A pool of moonshine comes and waits,
> but never waits long: the wind picks up
> loose gold like this and is gone.
> . . . .

> Homes for sandpipers — the script of their feet
> is on the sea shingles.
> . . . .

> Feathers and people in the crotch of a treetop
> Throw an evening waterfall of sleepy-songs.
> . . . .

> This handful of grass, brown, says little. This
> quarter-mile field of it, waving seeds ripening
> in the sun, a lake of luminous firefly lavender.

Some people have had difficulty in understanding Mr. Sandburg's rhythms, these long, slow
cadences, like the breath of air over an open moor.
Indeed, they are the very gift of the prairies, for
where else do we find them? Not in Whitman, not
in the Frenchmen, not among his contemporaries.
Mr. Sandburg's ear seldom fails; I can recall but

one instance of a false notation. In 'How Yesterday Looked,' occurs this stanza:

Ask me how the sunset looked on between the wind going
Down and the moon coming up and I would struggle
To tell the how of it.

This may be a typographical error, for the beat of the cadence requires the first line to end after 'looked on,' the second line after 'coming up,' and the rest of the stanza to be contained in the third line. But, even here, the error occurs merely in the break of the lines and not in the cadence *per se*.

I wish I had room to quote 'Silver Wind,' 'Crucible,' 'Tawny,' 'Sumach and Birds,' 'Far Rockaway Night till Morning,' 'North Atlantic,' 'Home Thoughts,' and the extraordinarily beautiful 'Haze.' Or, for a different reason, 'A.E.F.,' 'Accomplished Facts,' and even some few poems of 'the obsession' like 'People Who Must,' the terrible and dramatic 'White Hands,' the starkly ironical 'They Buy with an Eye to Looks,' the strange, pathetic 'Savoir Faire,' in which the poet parades his theories openly, but with an emotion which carries poetry in every line.

There is one thing we can say with Mr. Sandburg's three books in front of us. Either this is a very remarkable poet, or he is nothing, for with the minors he clearly has no place. He has greatly dared, and I personally believe that posterity, with its pruning hand, will mount him high on the ladder of poetic achievement.

THE POETRY OF D. H. LAWRENCE

'Look! We Have Come Through!' By D. H. Lawrence. New York: B. W. Huebsch.

WHEN one comes to think of it, the bringing over of the work of the writers of one country to another is determined in a singularly haphazard manner. As kissing goes by favour, so does this transatlantic transplanting. A publisher naturally issues what pleases him, or what he fondly imagines will please his public. He stands, therefore, to this public in somewhat the position of a schoolmaster. It is, after all, a sort of course of prescribed reading to which the general reader has access, and much that he might like to read he has no opportunity even to see, because, for one reason or another, the books have not been published in this country.

We, in America, know a certain section of English poetry well. Not to speak of the established names like Yeats and Masefield, or even of Rupert Brooke, we have become familiar with the poems of Walter de la Mare, of Siegfried Sassoon, of Francis Ledwidge, of Wilfred Wilson Gibson. We may think we are aware of all the divagations of modern English poetry, particularly if our knowledge include the work of such men as Richard

Aldington or Ralph Hodgson, but it is ten to one that most of us are ignorant of some poet of whom his countrymen think highly, but whom the accident of non-publication has kept from our knowledge. So true is this, that it is only very recently that the American reader has had a chance to read and know the work of a man who had attained a considerable fame in England even before the war. The man is D. H. Lawrence, novelist and poet.

It would be unfair not to acknowledge that some of Mr. Lawrence's books were issued in this country shortly after their publication in England. His greatest novel, 'Sons and Lovers,' although it never attained quite the recognition here that it did in England, was by no means ignored, and this is also true of his play 'The Widowing of Mrs. Holroyd.' But the man is not only dramatist and novel-writer, he is poet as well, having no less than four volumes to his credit. The first, 'Love Poems and Others,' bears the American imprint of Mitchell Kennerly; the second, 'Amores,' was published by B. W. Huebsch; the last, 'New Poems,' has only just appeared in London and it is too soon yet to look for it here; but the third book, 'Look! We Have Come Through!' has just been issued, again from the presses of Mr. B. W. Huebsch, who deserves to be greatly congratulated on his perspicacity in realizing its remarkable beauty and strength and making himself its American sponsor.

It should be interesting to American readers to learn something of a man who has made no little stir in England, and of whom Henry James thought well enough to consider among the very small handful of young writers whose work he analyses in his essay 'The New Novel' in 'Notes on Novelists.' Mr. Lawrence is more widely known as a novelist than as a poet; and no summary of his work can be complete which does not include both sides of his talent. But it is with his poetry that I am concerned at the moment, and particularly with 'Look! We Have Come Through!' although I shall give a few illustrations of his original peculiarities of style from the earlier books.

I know very little about Mr. Lawrence's life, a few facts merely. He is the descendant of a Huguenot family who fled the persecutions in France and settled in the Northern manufacturing district of England. His father was a miner, and I have reason to believe that his novel 'Sons and Lovers' is largely autobiographical. He won various scholarships at school, and his literary bent led him to become a schoolmaster. His first novel, 'The White Peacock,' issued in 1911, gained him immediate recognition; and shortly afterwards, in 1912, the appearance of 'The Trespasser' deepened

the impression made by the earlier book. Literature seemed to offer a promising career, and he
gave up teaching school. The high-water mark of
his reputation was reached on the publication of
'Sons and Lovers,' in 1913.

I do not know whether it was before or after the
appearance of this latter book that his health
broke down, but about this time he was obliged
to seek a milder climate, and went to live in Italy.

The outbreak of the war found him on a summer
visit to England, and it was impossible to return.
His health was in so precarious a state that there
was no question of the army. Since 1914 he has
lived in England, writing constantly. Three
volumes of poems, two novels, and a book of
Italian sketches have come from his pen in the last
four years.

Mr. Lawrence has thrown a gallant gauntlet to
Fate and with a smile, caught perhaps from his unflinching Huguenot ancestors.

Mr. Lawrence and his style are both perfectly
original and perfectly sincere. He has no prototype that I can find. He is a poet of sensation,
but of sensation as the bodily efflorescence of a
spiritual growth. Other poets have given us
sensuous images; other poets have spoken of love
as chiefly desire; but in no other poet does desire
seem so surely the 'outward and visible form of an

inward and spiritual grace.' Mr. Lawrence does not do this by obscuring passion in a poetical subterfuge, he gives the naked desire as it is; but so tuned is his mind that it is always the soul made visible in a supreme moment. In the last two stanzas of 'Lilies in the Fire,' he says:

With the swiftest fire of my love, you are destroyed.
'Tis degradation deep to me, that my best
Soul's whitest lightning which should bright attest
God stepping down to earth in one white stride,

Means only to you a clogged, numb burden of flesh
Heavy to bear, even heavy to uprear
Again from earth, like lilies wilted sere
Flagged on the floor, that before stood up so fresh.

Mr. Lawrence has been spoken of as an erotic poet, and that is true, but it is only one half of the truth; for his eroticism leans always to the mystic something of which it is an evidence. Not to understand this is to fail completely to comprehend the whole meaning of his work.

I shall come back to this presently in speaking of his last book, but now I want to turn for a moment to other sides of his genius, for I do not hesitate to declare Mr. Lawrence to be a man of genius. He does not quite get his genius into harness, the cart of his work frequently overturns or goes awry, but it is no less Pegasus who draws it, even if Mr. Lawrence is not yet an entirely proficient charioteer.

Professor Lowes once employed a happy phrase of George Meredith's to describe the Imagists. It was: 'Men lying on their backs, flying imagination like a kite.' Mr. Lawrence possesses a soaring kite, and all nature lets loose the string. Let me take a few lines at random from various poems which show how truly he possesses the poet's twin gifts of sight and expression:

> The morning breaks like a pomegranate
> In a shining crack of red.
> .   .   .   .
>
> ... the festoon
> Of the sky sagged dusty as a spider cloth,
> And coldness clogged the sea.
> .   .   .   .
>
> Slowly the moon is rising out of the ruddy haze,
> Divesting herself of her golden shift, and so
> Emerging white and exquisite.
> .   .   .   .
>
> The wind comes from the north
> Blowing little flocks of birds
> Like spray across the town.
> .   .   .   .
>
> A yellow leaf from the darkness
> Hops like a frog before me.
> .   .   .   .
>
> The moon is broken in twain, and half a moon
> Before me lies on the still, pale floor of the sky.

Those are evidences of visual imagination; now let us see how he manages auditory:

The moon-mist is over the village, out of the mist speaks the bell,
And all the little roofs of the village bow low, pitiful, beseeching, resigned:
Oh, little home, what is it I have not done well?
Ah, suddenly I love you,
As I hear the sharp clear trot of a pony down the road,
Succeeding sharp little sounds dropping into silence,
Clear upon the long-drawn hoarseness of a train down the valley.

Notice how well the first lines give the stillness, the hush of a quiet night, and how suddenly it is shattered by the quick beating of the pony's hoofs.

Mr. Lawrence is also the possessor of a most vivid colour sense, witness this little piece:

GREEN

The dawn was apple-green,
    The sky was green wine held up in the sun,
The moon was a golden petal between.

She opened her eyes, and green
    They shone, clear like flowers undone
For the first time, now for the first time seen.

That poem will show Mr. Lawrence's original blending of free rhythms with metrical form. He seldom writes *vers libre*, although in 'Look! We

Have Come Through!' he seems to be leaning more toward it, but this poetry which the pedants say 'will not scan' is almost as much of a distinct form. In other hands, I fear the results would be excruciating; in Mr. Lawrence's, some happy instinct causes the jars in the metre to become an added beauty.

This queer use of metrical verse may almost be styled an invention, but one feels that it came to Mr. Lawrence inevitably, while he was pursuing something else, for there never was a poet more bent upon saying things, and less concerned with mere beauty of trapping. This beauty, which he has in abundance, is innate.

Mr. Lawrence makes no compromise with stark and violent truth. He sees life as a war between the dull and the visionary. Here are two characters. They love, but cannot understand each the other; it is a theme he comes back to again and again:

FIREFLIES IN THE CORN

A Woman taunts her Lover

Look at the little darlings in the corn!
The rye is taller than you, who think yourself
So high and mighty: look how its heads are borne
Dark and proud in the sky, like a number of knights
Passing with spears and pennants and manly scorn.

And always likely! — Oh, if I could ride
With my head held high-serene against the sky
Do you think I'd have a creature like you at my side
With your gloom and your doubt that you love me?
   O darling rye,
How I adore you for your simple pride!

And those bright fireflies wafting in between
And over the swaying cornstalks, just above
All their dark-feathered helmets, like little green
Stars come low and wandering here for love
Of this dark earth, and wandering all serene —!

How I adore you, you happy things, you dears
Riding the air and carrying all the time
Your little lanterns behind you: it cheers
My heart to see you settling and trying to climb
The cornstalks, tipping with fire their spears.

All over the corn's dim motion, against the blue
Dark sky of night, the wandering glitter, the swarm
Of questing brilliant things: — you joy, you true
Spirit of careless joy: ah, how I warm
My poor and perished soul at the joy of you!

The Man answers and she mocks
   You're a fool, woman. I love you and you know I do!
     — Lord, take his love away, it makes him whine.
   And I give you everything that you want me to.
     — Lord, dear Lord, do you think he ever *can* shine?

'Look! We Have Come Through!' is an amazing
book. It is to my mind a greater novel even than

'Sons and Lovers,' for all that it is written in a rather disconnected series of poems. The 'Foreword' and the 'Argument' tell the story:

FOREWORD

These poems should not be considered separately, as so many single pieces. They are intended as an essential story, or history, or confession, unfolding one from the other in organic development, the whole revealing the intrinsic experience of a man during the crisis of manhood, when he marries and comes into himself. The period covered is, roughly, the sixth lustre of a man's life.

ARGUMENT

After much struggling and loss in love and in the world of man, the protagonist throws in his lot with a woman who is already married. Together they go into another country, she perforce leaving her children behind. The conflict of love and hate goes on between the man and the woman, and between these two and the world around them, till it reaches some sort of conclusion, they transcend into some condition of blessedness.

Beautiful as the individual poems are, it is only when one reads the book from the first page to the last that one realizes the extraordinary truth, the naked simplicity and vigour, of it. I dislike the expression 'human document,' it is so often employed to designate vulgar outpourings of no real merit, but if we forget its abuse for a moment, this is the only term to apply to Mr. Lawrence's book. It is sorrow made flesh. It is courage 'coming through.' It is illusion, disillusion, mounting at last to vision, to a humble, even a grateful, acceptance of life.

It is impossible to give any adequate idea of this book by quotation. Still, perhaps the drift may be intimated by two poems. One, in the midst of the struggle:

HISTORY

The listless beauty of the hour
When snow fell on the apple trees
And the wood-ash gathered in the fire
And we faced our first miseries.

Then the sweeping sunshine of noon
When the mountains like chariot cars
Were ranked to blue battle — and you and I
Counted our scars.

And then in a strange, grey hour
We lay mouth to mouth, with your face
Under mine like a star on the lake,
And I covered the earth, and all space.

The silent, drifting hours
Of morn after morn
And night drifting up to the night
Yet no pathway worn.

> Your life, and mine, my love
> Passing on and on, the hate
> Fusing closer and closer with love
> Till at length they mate.

One, when the struggle is at last resolving into peace:

SONG OF A MAN WHO HAS COME THROUGH

Not I, not I, but the wind that blows through me!
A fine wind is blowing the new direction of Time.
If only I let it bear me, carry me, if only it carry me!
If only I am sensitive, subtle, oh, delicate, a winged gift!
If only, most lovely of all, I yield myself and am borrowed
By the fine, fine wind that takes its course through the chaos of the world
Like a fine, an exquisite chisel, a wedge-blade inserted;
If only I am keen and hard like the sheer tip of a wedge
Driven by invisible blows,
The rock will split, we shall come at the wonder, we shall find the Hesperides.

Oh, for the wonder that bubbles into my soul,
I would be a good fountain, a good well-head,
Would blur no whisper, spoil no expression.

What is the knocking?
What is the knocking at the door in the night?
It is somebody wants to do us harm.

No, no, it is the three strange angels.
Admit them, admit them.

It is difficult to analyse dispassionately the poetry in a volume so full of travail. The bitterness, the anguish, the hard clarity, of the revelation all disarm us. The poems are born in a rush of passionate eloquence, and they are poetry because the man who wrote them is a poet, not because he has been at pains to make them so.

As a book, the volume is a masterpiece; as poetry, perhaps it is not quite that. Art is not raw fact. Poetry cannot rise into its rightful being as the highest of all arts if it be tied down to the coarse material of bald, even if impassioned, truth. Truth has its own beauty, but it is not the beauty of poetry. In the greatest poets, the two go, or seem to go, hand in hand, for the highest poetry is also the most simple. Sappho's 'I loved you once, Atthis' gives us this shock of poetry and truth in one. Dante, Shakespeare, have no fear of losing passion by transmuting it into poetry. In Mr. Lawrence's case, the God-given spark of poetry in the man often saves him, and yet, as poetry, the volume fails by a too loud insistence upon one thing, by an almost neurotic beating, beating, upon the same tortured note. It is not because the effect of the volume is over-sensual, for we have seen how Mr. Lawrence regards the sensual; it is because of the way in which it is done. 'Look! We Have Come Through!' is all the more a 'human document,' perhaps, because it is unbalanced; but on that very account it falls short of being the immortal poetry it might have been.

Yet, after all, who are we to say what is or what is not 'immortal'? Mr. Lawrence, in spite of his inclusion in the Imagist Anthologies, cannot be confined within the boundaries of any school. His is realism, but not the realism of Masefield or Gibson; his is romance, but not the romance of de la Mare or James Stephens; his is simplicity, but scarcely that charming *fausse naïveté* of Hodgson; his is nature and flowers and fields, but not the nature of Siegfried Sassoon. He is neither worldling nor rustic. He has none of the weary culture of Rupert Brooke, nor has he the cosmopolitan tolerance of James Elroy Flecker. He sounds an original note in English poetry, and is unconcerned with his originality. So occupied is he to express what is in him that his manner is inevitable. He studies no tricks of difference, he simply is different. Sincere, loyal, serious, strong, permeated with beauty, scored upon by tragedy, he is himself and no other. We may like him or dislike him, but we cannot ignore him if we would know the full circle cf English poetry to-day.

A VOICE CRIES IN OUR WILDERNESS

'Touch and Go.' By D. H. Lawrence. New York: Thomas Seltzer.

To those of us who admire the work of D. H. Lawrence his comparative neglect by the larger reading public is a matter of surprise. When, some years ago, his 'Sons and Lovers' appeared, Mr. Lawrence was immediately accorded by his countrymen a place among the first of the younger novelists, but for some unknown reason America failed to appreciate that remarkable book. Why? Perhaps its stark and rather terrible power frightened a public who could read 'Pollyanna' without nausea; perhaps the very truth to locality discouraged Americans who knew nothing of industrial life in the Midlands, so very different from anything we have here; perhaps the dialect was hard of comprehension; perhaps a thousand things, among others its belated publication on this side of the ocean; but the fact remains that Americans never discovered D. H. Lawrence until the ridiculous and unfair suppression of 'The Rainbow,' on the mere technicality of an obsolescent law, brought him an undeserved notoriety and oblivion.

'The Rainbow' was not a particularly good book. I hear it is to be reissued in England, but whether it is or not matters little to the total effect of Mr. Lawrence's work. It is true that 'Sons and Lovers' still remains his high-water mark, but I believe that to be largely the fault of conditions. The tragedy of the war, from which no artist in the European countries has come unscathed, is one of these conditions; the other I believe to be the cold shoulder of neglect. 'The Prussian Officer, and Other Stories' was unhappily named considering the moment of its appearance, and, although it preceded 'The Rainbow,' it was little read. If the very people who were estranged by its title had taken the pains to look at the first story, from which this title was derived, they would have found as scathing a denunciation of the military system as could well be.

But Mr. Lawrence is not only a writer of novels, he is a poet and dramatist as well. He has published five volumes of poetry, so passionate, so mystical, so original in form and thought that, failing to fit into any of the contemporary niches, he has been passed over by all the little Johnny-look-in-the-airs gaping for a genius they can understand.

In one respect, Mr. Lawrence is like Blake. To him, sex is mystical and divine; he explains this again and again, or rather, he expresses it, and behold, a low-pitched world misunderstands, as long ago their forebears misunderstood Blake. Both Blake and Mr. Lawrence have a message, but neither the one nor the other speaks in terms which the majority of readers find it easy to translate. A year ago, in these pages, I tried to make this clear in a review of his searching and sad volume, 'Look! We Have Come Through!' I had little hope of succeeding where the author himself had not succeeded, but at least I could strip his message away from his beautiful and obscuring verse, and set it in words of one syllable. Perhaps Mr. Lawrence's poetry is for the few, as Blake's has always been. Mysticism is hardly comprehended in this our America to-day. But Mr. Lawrence's poems are not his novels, nor yet his plays; we must seek another reason for the neglect of these.

Mr. Lawrence's chief characteristic is sincerity. He says what he thinks and he thinks a very great deal. An excessively sensitive man, things hurt him profoundly, he is raw from contacts which have excoriated his soul. He longs desperately for beauty and peace, for a social order in which men shall seek out one another's virtues, and do each for his neighbor beyond that neighbor's need. But when I say that Mr. Lawrence thinks a great deal, I do not mean to imply that his thought is concerned with exact systems of reformation. Remember, he is an artist, not a political economist. He has thought enough to distrust panaceas, and, mystic as he is, he is no half one. Like his great forerunners, he knows that man's institutions will change only when men's hearts change. His is no jejune cry for this or that minor alteration; it is a voice of sorrow lamenting the waywardness of the world. He speaks to a wilderness of blind reactionaries and fussy, discontented agitators. He speaks in the guise of a story or a play, and few heed him, for no one likes to be reminded that the Kingdom of God is in one's own heart. Tom, Dick, and Harry, each striving to comprehend and be just to the other two, and where would be the need of reform? But this method is not popular, has never been so less than now, when no one can take a step along the Kingdom's road without banding with some dozens of his fellows and calling the group the society for the suppression of something or other. We dote upon suppressions, for that always means that some one else is to be suppressed. Who wrote the old, trenchant couplet, which speaks of such persons as men who

> Compound with sins they are inclined to
> By damning those they have no mind to?

How natural, when, by personality or circumstance, you are not like the other fellow, and his ways annoy you, to suppress him! Very natural, but scarcely, perhaps, wise. Since you, and I, and the other fellow, have all got to live together in one world, we might — in fact, in all common sense, we should — strive to find out how to do it. What boots it to kill the other fellow, since a thousand of his genus will assuredly rise up to avenge the murder? This is true in the private, individual life; it is also true in the great group life, the body politic. And here we have Mr. Lawrence's pre-occupation in a nutshell. 'Look! We Have Come Through!' is concerned with the struggle of two individual natures; 'Touch and Go,' his new play, shows this struggle forcing itself into the conscious-ness of the two great group divisions in modern society — Capital and Labour.

Since an artist works, not directly by argument and explanation, but deviously, by parables, Mr. Lawrence has set a preface in front of his play as a sort of Greek chorus. This preface is so excellent, so much in the manner of the great English tra-dition, in this case the tradition of Swift, Stern, Lamb, Hazlitt, that it holds, and urges, and ends by being, I think, even better than the play, a fine little masterpiece of eight pages. Personally, I should like to print it, and give it away as a hand-bill to all and sundry in the streets.

One cannot pick lines out of a perfectly written thing and keep it alive, and yet I must give a little of this preface. In the first place, it should be stated that this play is one of a series entitled 'Plays for a People's Theatre.' To dash into the middle, then:

A People's Theatre. Note the indefinite article. It isn't The People's Theatre, but A People's Theatre. Not The people: il popolo, le peuple, das Volk, this monster is the same the world over: Plebs, the proletariat. Not the Theatre of Plebs, the proletariat, but the theatre of A People. What people? Quel peuple donc? — A People's Theatre... Since we can't produce it, let us deduce it. Major premise: the seats are cheap. Minor premise: the plays are good...

The seats are cheap. That has a nasty proletarian look about it. But appearances are deceptive. The proletariat isn't poor. Everybody is poor except Capital and Labour. Between these upper and nether mill-stones great numbers of decent people are squeezed... The plays of a people's theatre are plays about people.

It doesn't look much at first sight. After all — people! Yes, people! Not *the people*, *i.e.* Plebs, nor yet the Upper Ten. People. Neither Piccoli nor Grandi in our republic. People.

People, ah God! Not mannequins.... Men who are somebody, not men who are something.

Then out of the irony and the truth comes at last his premise:

Granted that men are still men, Labour *v.* Capitalism

is a tragic struggle... In Shakespeare's time it was the people *versus* king storm that was brewing... Now a new wind is getting up... We say it is a mere material struggle, a money-grabbing affair. But this is only one aspect of it... The conflict is in pure, passionate antagonism turning upon the poles of belief. Majesty was only *hors d'œuvres* to this tragic repast.

After detailing the attitude of the two contending parties, he asks, answers:

What's the solution? There is no solution. But still there is a choice. There's a choice between a mess and a tragedy.

He tells us that tragedy is a profound struggle for something coming to life, a struggle to bring a new freedom, a creative activity in which death is a climax in the progression towards new being, and goes on:

Therefore, if we could but comprehend or feel the tragedy in the great labour struggle, the intrinsic tragedy of having to pass through death to birth, our souls would still know some happiness, the very happiness of creative suffering. Instead of which we pile accident on accident, we tear the fabric of our existence fibre by fibre, we confidently look forward to the time when the whole structure will come down on our heads. Yet after all that, when we are squirming under the débris, we shall have no more faith or hope or satisfaction than we have now....

Is that all? Not quite. There is the Kingdom,

implied in the preface, more nearly stated in the play. For, perhaps rightly, Mr. Lawrence believes:

Therefore we should open our hearts. For one thing, we should have a People's Theatre. Perhaps it would help us in this hour of confusion better than anything.

And so we reach the play, prepared to see in action, hope, tragedy, a series of clues, but scarcely the end to which they lead.

We are introduced to a family of mine-owners. The father, now superseded in his management of the mine by his son, has early in life become haunted by the disproportion in the lives of masters and men. Benevolent and just, he has spent himself in trying to better the conditions of his colliers, and, obedient principally to his philanthropic nature, has let things run at a rather loose end from a business point of view. While still young, this gentleman had married a woman of a shrewd, uncompromising type, who sees her husband's labours, year after year, taken for granted by his work-people, who have come to regard his care of them first as their due and later as an inadequate return for their services. Embittered by this spectacle, which her husband refuses to recognize, the poor lady has gradually lost her mental balance, until hatred of the colliers has become a very part of her deep love for her husband, now old and ill.

The son returns from abroad, and from an unfortunate love-affair, to assume control of the mines. He is an energetic, hard man, who, finding things considerably down at heel, undertakes to improve them by instituting drastic reforms of management and expenditure. The colliers, egged on by demagogues, resent the new order, and the ferment has reached an ugly limit when the play begins.

The lady from whom Gerald Barlow (the son) has parted, seeks him out, and they come together again in a strained and worrying relation. In these two characters and their dependent attraction and antagonism, Mr. Lawrence symbolizes the larger situation. It is a lighter tragedy playing over and illuminating the greater.

The climax of an impossible condition is reached when the office force demands a raise in pay. Gerald, annoyed at the threat of a strike of the colliers in sympathy with the clerks, declares he will not be bullied and refuses. Unhappily, a parley with a delegate of the men, Job Arthur Freer, coming after a harrowing scene of nagging and misunderstanding with Anabel, breaks Gerald's control, and he knocks Job Arthur down and kicks him. Later, Job Arthur incites the men to violence. Gerald is taken from his motor, and, in sight of Anabel, is maltreated and nearly killed, because he refuses to say why he will not give the raise to the clerks. A friend intervenes, and persuades the men to let him get up, promising that he shall answer. The consequent parley, and the friend's efforts at mediation, is the finest moment in the play. After the terrible scene in which Gerald Barlow is spread-eagled on the ground and beaten, Oliver (the friend) appeals to the men:

> Can't you see it's no good, either side? It's no mortal use. We might as well all die to-morrow, or to-day, or this minute, as go on bullying the other side, and the other side bullying back. We'd all *better* die.

And again:

> You see, if you wanted to arrange things so that money flowed more naturally, so that it flowed naturally to every man, according to his needs, I think we could all soon agree. But you don't. What you want is to take it away from one set and give it to another — or keep it yourselves.

The men are hardly placated, and when Oliver says, 'I'm sure the owners would agree with you,' they are both astonished and skeptical, but Gerald admits that he too wants 'a better way.' Taken aback by this, the miners scarcely realize when he says, 'Now I'm going.' Growling, but already on the way to obey an accustomed au-

thority, some voices shout, 'Who says goin'?'
But Gerald goes, telling them, 'About this affair
here we'll cry quits; no more said about it. About
a new way of life, a better way all round — I tell
you I want it and need it as much as ever you do.
I don't care about money really. But I'm never
going to be bullied.' A voice asks incredulously,
'Who doesn't care about money?' To which
Gerald replies, 'I don't. I think we ought to be
able to alter the whole system — but not by bully-
ing, not because one lot wants what the other has
got.' Another voice jeers, 'No, because you have
got everything.' Gerald, resuming his lost control,
'Where's my coat? Now then, step out of the
way.' Apparently they do, and the play ends.

This is not the strike situation as we know it in
America. This final scene could never be enacted
except by men of the same race, which our miners
and mine-owners never are. But we must suppose
it true to type, as Mr. Lawrence was brought up in
the mine fields. He is of them, brain and bone.
Mr. Lawrence has been fair in making his mine-
owner almost as pig-headed a brute as any of his
men; his kicking Job Arthur is probably typically
true, but it is revolting, quite as revolting as the
final scene of Job Arthur's revenge. But mere
matters of local behaviour have nothing to do with
the central theme of the play, which is a portrayal

of the furious forces standing in the way of re-
generation. Doubt as we may about the ultimate
effect of this parley on Gerald or on the men,
the fundamental antagonism which underlies the
economic *impasse* to-day is well presented, and,
Utopian as it undoubtedly appears, who believes
that Mr. Lawrence's hint at a solution does not
point the way, if only it were workable? Mr. Lawrence has courageously uttered a truth which will
be popular with neither side, largely because it is
the stark truth, but also because men in a passion
have sealed ears.

JOHN MASEFIELD

'Reynard the Fox, or The Ghost Heath Run.' By John Masefield. New York: The Macmillan Company.

SINCE the publication of 'Rosas,' many of Mr. Masefield's admirers have felt, somewhat sadly, that they must not expect another 'Everlasting Mercy' or 'Dauber' from his pen, that the poet had done his best work and that what was likely to follow would probably not add much to his fame. 'Reynard the Fox' is not another 'Dauber'; but neither, thank Fortune, is it another 'Rosas.' If the new volume shows us no new vein for the first time tapped, it proves how rich the old vein still is.

Masefield is like one of his own thoroughbred hunters. We know his literary ancestry, and he runs true to type. There is no more English Englishman than John Masefield; he is bone, and mind, and sinew of the British Isles. I do not know how it may be with our heterogeneous American public, but to one of the same blood, how distant soever it be, to find so pure a specimen of the breed still following the old line with the old clear-eyed vision brings a sense of satisfaction bordering on thankfulness.

Cosmopolitanism is good, but race is better. I do not believe in an art which is not rooted in the soil, even though that soil be merely the rusty pavement of a city street. One may write of ancient Egypt or the music of the spheres; but, if one is any good, that writing is all tinged by the colour of the earth one walks on. Could Shakespeare be anything but an Englishman, Dante an Italian? Is not Heine very Jew of Jews, and Molière Paris to its finest edge of irony?

But Masefield is not only an Englishman; he is a throw-back to an older, vanished England. Yet, also, he is very modern, he is modern man in his psychological reactions, he is modern man in his pity, his stern resolve to face life's cruelty and bitterness with no comforting plaster of lies spread upon it.

The war has hurt Mr. Masefield. I do not mean that it has hurt his art, but that it has hurt his mind, his spirit. He has given us no bitter invectives; that is not his way. Instead, he is cast back, pitifully, achingly, upon the world he once knew, and that he deeply loved. I have not been to England since the war, but I am told that it is changed almost beyond belief. For better? for worse? Time alone will tell. But different it must be. This latest volume of his, which, from the publisher's announcement on the slip-cover, one would suppose was merely a rollicking tale of the hunting-field, is really a cry of hunger for the past, a wave of nostalgic longing for the old, simple, thoughtless days of security and peace.

Not that I imagine that sport will ever be banished from the English country-side. While the race of Britons last, there will be sport, even the cruel sport of chasing foxes to death in the longest, most lingering, and most brutal manner possible. For the English, who love animals better than any other nation has ever done, seem to lose all power of imagination when sport is in question. The horror of the English huntsman in Ireland who, having been told by a native that he knew where a fox was to be found, and that said fox would be forthcoming on the payment of a consideration, suddenly discovered that the Irishman proposed to sell his tame fox for the run, is typical. It is 'unsportsmanlike,' utterly unthinkable and abominable, to hunt a fox who has been reared to believe men his friends. Where a wild fox is concerned, the imagination simply goes to sleep. This is not hypocrisy; it is atrophy. Mr. Masefield (although I can scarcely believe him addicted to fox-hunting in his own person) shares this racial feeling. He follows his fox through a long run, and then, having in some sort made friends with him, he simply cannot kill him. So the hounds are made to follow a new scent, and the fox they finally kill is left un-personified to us, a mere *thing*, as it were, while our particular, known Reynard escapes.

Fox-hunting may last in England for all time, but will it? If the land is cut up? If non-hunting folk have innumerable fenced-in garden-patches? If the pace of life becomes as rapid as it is in this country, for instance? We have many foxes in America, but how few regular hunts! One pack I know has recently been given up, and is it a soli-tary instance?

I believe all this to have been in Masefield's mind when he wrote his book. England, patri-archal and dearly loved England, changing as the sky changes with the mounting hours of day. Homesick, weary, he thinks of the old, gay, re-curring happenings of his woods, and fields, and downs, of that country he has looked upon so often.

If one wanted to give England in a nutshell, there are two big fields to work in — England in her own country-side, and English ships on all the seas of the globe. But, in the first place, Mr. Masefield has done amply well by ships; in the second, it is just the country-side to which his heart turns in its sadness and longing. The line of a hill sharp on the sky, the feather-light softness of woods along the flank of it, how a certain pond goes blue from a turn of road, the sound of a church

bell always heard like that when there is going to
be a frost.

So he calls up his country, the dear, jocund,
pre-war country that was his home, as one calls
back a childhood pleasure in the midst of sorrow.
Not that the book is sad. It is quite the opposite.
Probably nine people out of ten will agree with the
publisher's jacket, but the tenth will find it only
the more charming for the hint of wistfulness which
runs through it from beginning to end.

This is a long preamble, but it really contains the
whole thing. What does it matter in what style a
love-letter be written, so that every line is charged
with feeling. 'Reynard the Fox' is so charged,
and that fact keeps us galloping with the horses
through one hundred and sixty-six pages of much
the same thing with barely a thought of fatigue.

In fact, I should go farther and say that only in
one section does the sense of length consciously
obtrude, and that is in the description of the people who come to the meet. Poe was very wise and
told a solid truth when he said that all long poems
are composed of moments of high emotion joined
together by arid stretches. Mr. Masefield has ar-
ranged his poem with exquisite care. He has so
altered and diversified its texture from time to
time as to keep the whole moving with an amazing
sense of rapidity. I can recall no poem of his which

seems to me so well ordered as this. It begins immediately; it ends swiftly and satisfactorily. It is a work of high art, a vivid picture of a place and time, a strongly imagined dream of memory. It is not, perhaps, of the inner courts of poetry. Chaucer did the sort of thing infinitely better, and no one has yet come near him in the *genre*. Sir Walter Scott strutted in it; Crabbe hobbled about it; Shelley, Coleridge, Keats threw it off altogether; but Masefield returns to it, retrieves it. He cannot equal Chaucer, but it is almost a shame to whisper his cousinship to Scott and Crabbe, so far is he beyond them.

If the lines at times seem only not prose because they are rhymed and metred, there are others so beautiful as to be worth much waiting. The rhythm is forthright and lusty, but it must be admitted that the couplets jangle heavily, line to line, with a rather interminable monotony. Any one who has heard Mr. Masefield read his poems aloud must recognize that rhythm to him is merely a visual pattern. His reading has no swing, no sense of fluid and relieving movements. This seems a pity, for octosyllabics lend themselves to such delightful phrasings. Think of Keats's 'Eve of Saint Mark,' and then read anywhere you please in 'Reynard the Fox,' and you will scarcely believe that the two poets are working in the same

medium. The immense speed of the run in Mr.
Masefield's poem is not achieved by rhythm but
through the poignance of idea. We know, we have
long known, what Mr. Masefield cannot do; what
he has done is to write stories in verse which are
so interesting that people who have no taste for
poetry cannot lay them down, and which, in spite
of all the things they lack, at least have so many
beauties of observation and phrase (in his best
work) that even the most fastidious amateurs of
the art are forced to an ungrudging admiration.

'Reynard the Fox' begins with a delightful
abruptness:

> The meet was at 'The Cock and Pye
> By Charles and Martha Enderby,'
> The grey, three-hundred-year-old inn
> Long since the haunt of Benjamin
> The highwayman, who rode the bay.
> The tavern fronts the coaching way,
> The mail changed horses there of old.
> It has a strip of grassy mould
> In front of it, a broad green strip.

The description of the inn is amplified until the
stables are reached — the stables, early on a hunting morning. All this passage about the horses
and grooms is one of the nicest in the book. Perhaps one must have been brought up in a stable to
get the full glow of it. The smell of leather, and oil,

and ammonia, the sounds of horses munching, the bang of the feed-box lids, the creak and groan of the pump,

> ... the soft
> Hay's scratching slither down the shoot.
> Then with a thud some horse's foot
> Stamped, and the gulping munch again
> Resumed its lippings at the grain.

For me too, this is memory. It must be so to many people in this increasingly horseless age. It is a solace to read it; I know it was as a solace that he wrote it.

The followers of the hunt begin to arrive, and with them comes the only really dull part of the poem. There are a lot of these people, and each is stupider than the last. Undoubtedly it is a *tour de force* to have created so many; but, since they are only superficially sketched, the creative power has not been very painfully taxed. Here is no such effort of the imagination as Mr. Masters had to make when he conceived 'Spoon River'; no such carefully worked psychology, drawing on the threads of innumerable contacts to weave its figures, as Chaucer displayed. These followers of the hunt are very much in the rough, and I think the reason is not far to seek. Mr. Masefield can depict men when he chooses, he has abundantly proved so much; this time, consciously or unconsciously, he did not choose. His hunt is not a character study, it is a symbolical treatment of the theme of 'home.' The poet is immensely concerned with the ground over which his hunt gallops, with the skies under which the chase is run. These he remembers, these he wants to preserve for his bitter comfort. I do not believe that he himself hunts. Of course I may be wrong, but it does not seem to fit, somehow. Therefore, in choosing a hunt to symbolize his rural England, he gives it best where he has personally come in touch with it. He has watched hunts sweep by time and again, probably, but that he has hobnobbed with the throng gathered at the meets, I very much doubt. Therefore his people are typical, not individual, and it would be almost too much to expect seventy-two typical individuals to be interesting. They are brought in to play the rôle of rural English population, and doubtless they are well-chosen samples of the kind, but Mr. Masefield is at scant pains to do more than catalogue them. The real actor of the drama is the land itself. Interest wakes again, never afterwards to flag, in the arrival of the hounds:

> But now the clock had struck the hour,
> And round the corner, down the road
> The bob-bob-bobbing serpent flowed
> With three black knobs upon its spine;
> Three bobbing black-caps in a line.

So enter, in most intriguing fashion, the huntsman and the two whips. We are as eager as the
folk before the inn:

> There was a general turn of faces,
> The men and horses shifted places,
> And round the corner came the hunt,
> Those feathery things, the hounds, in front.

The hunt repairs to Ghost Heath Wood, which
the dogs are set to draw, and the first part ends
just as an old hound gives tongue and the hunt
proper begins.

It is this second part which is the glory of the
book. The swiftness of that run is amazing. Good
hunts have been written before, but in prose, and
this is poetry, from the first page to the last. The
first part of the poem frequently betrays a prose
attack; the second part, never.

No, Mr. Masefield is clearly no hunter. This
poem was written by a man who has observed
horses, but seldom ridden them. You hear and
see what an onlooker might hear and see, what a
poet might imagine to have been. But there is no
glazed leather and moving muscle between Mr.
Masefield's knees throughout this hunt. He feels
the wind as the fox felt it, not as the rider would.
He takes his fences from the flat ground along the
hedge, the horses rise to the jump, but he does not

rise with them, jamming on his hat, lifting his
hunter, heaving back in his saddle at the crest.
His jumps are visual sensation, not organic. Not
that he commits solecisms. I have not found one,
except in a few names of stable gear, which may
be different in England from what they are in
America, and the somewhat strange act of polish-
ing stirrups before a hunt instead of immediately
after the last one. No, the matter is not one of
mistakes; it is the far more subtle one of memory
and feeling.

Actuated perhaps by this feeling, more probably
for the sake of contrast and the great pity that is
the man, Mr. Masefield takes his hunt from the
point of view of the fox. And here occur passages
of unforgettable beauty:

> And foxes lie on short-grassed turf,
> Nose between paws, to hear the surf
> Of wind in the beeches drowsily.
> .   .   .   .

> The wind was westerly but still;
> The sky a high fair-weather cloud,
> Like meadows ridge-and-furrow ploughed,
> Just glinting sun but scarcely moving.
> Blackbirds and thrushes thought of loving,
> Catkins were out; the day seemed tense
> It was so still.
> .   .   .   .

> ... Larches, black to the sky,
> A sadness breathing with one long sigh,

> Grey ghosts of trees under funeral plumes,
> A mist of twig over soft brown glooms.

Have larches ever been better described?
The fox goes

> — up wind like an April thrush.
>
> .   .   .   .
>
> The kestrel cruising over meadow
> Watched the hunt gallop on his shadow.
>
> .   .   .   .
>
> They saw the water snaking slim
> Ahead, like silver.

Such lines as these make up for a good deal of rather forced diction throughout the poem. Obsolete words are dragged from their peaceful obscurity and thrust into the light, sometimes to tag a rhyme, sometimes for no apparent reason. Cows become 'kye' on occasion, a plough 'drave,' but the worst of all is the middle-English 'newe,' on page 49, with the mute 'e' sounded as in the French from which it was taken. Doubtless these things are a fault of taste, or would be except that I believe them to go deeper than that. They are, again, the unconscious tribute to the land of a long descent and its usages. I do not believe the poet sought them; I do think he had not the heart to turn them away when they came, for the sake of auld lang syne.

In other cases, words are coined for purposes of

onomatopœia, a device of which the poem is full;
the horses 'trit-trot,' the pump goes 'ker-lump,
ker-lump.' Sometimes, however, these inventions
or returns to ancient usage are extremely happy,
as when a blackbird calls with a 'chackering
scattering cry,' or 'Six hens cluckered and flucked
to perch,' or 'The horses cocked and pawed and
whickered.'

The hunt itself is magnificent. Valleys and
downland roll beneath us. Villages, copses,
brooks, with their queer, twisted English names,
flash out of the green distance and disappear behind. It is England indeed, England unwinding
from a quickly twisting spool. For we are running with the fox, or, checked for a moment,
straying with the questing hounds.

Hardly as fine as the 'Dauber' — well, we can
admit that, and yet leave a great margin of ful-
filment. If 'Reynard the Fox' is not Mr. Masefield's best work, it ranks but little below it. For
sheer excitement and suspense, the poem is without its equal in English poetry, so far as I know,
unless one can possibly compare it to 'The Ancient
Mariner,' with which it has not another point of
contact. As poetry, it again does not reach the
'Dauber,' but it has its own beauty, as I have
shown, and of this beauty, and because to most
readers it will be the haunting loveliness which is

England, I will set down these lines as at once motto and valedictory:

> Some grey cathedral in a town
> Where drowsy bells toll out the time
> To shaven closes sweet with lime,
> And wall-flower roots drive out the mortar
> All summer in the Norman Dortar.

AN UNFORTUNATE INTERLUDE

'King Cole.' By John Masefield. New York: The Macmillan Company.

MR. MASEFIELD is writing too much; that is one's chief impression on finishing his last book, 'King Cole.' His creative faculty is like a beast within him, evidently, always crying out for something it may work upon. One can imagine him seeking high and low for a subject which will still this devouring, eager dæmon for a while, finding it superbly at times, at others not really finding it at all, but cheating both himself and the dæmon with some pinchbeck trifle stumbled upon in the hunt.

The artistic dæmon is an odd animal; with all the will in the world, he cannot function properly with inadequate material. And by 'inadequate material' I do not mean what you or I might consider inadequate, but what the dæmon finds to be so. The dæmon does its best, of course (the dæmons of well-trained artists seldom sulk), and Mr. Masefield does his best, but the silk purse which should have been, remains, when all is said and done, a most recalcitrant sow's ear.

'King Cole' is not one of Mr. Masefield's star volumes. To borrow the resourceful Mr. Baedeker's admirable system for a moment, let us think of these volumes as starred, double-starred, and with no star at all. 'The Everlasting Mercy,' 'The Widow in the Bye Street,' 'Reynard the Fox' — every reader will double-star these, and, if the system permits of triple starring, 'Dauber' will surely receive the extra accolade. I shall not follow the single stars and no stars here; it would take my whole paper. Let me say, then, simply, that 'King Cole' is in the no-star category, an undistinguished member of a noble company, a reproduction of a fine pattern, but, in itself, merely an uninspired copy.

'King Cole' is a dull and commonplace story; at least I find it so. That is not criticism, I admit, but preference, and preference is neither here nor there. Still, if we approach this matter of dullness backwards, through its antitheses, and see what 'King Cole' might have been, perhaps we shall have a clew to what it is not.

The main theme is stated at the beginning of the poem. The legendary monarch King Cole, after leading an exemplary life, dies. But 'exemplary' hardly gives the measure of his virtue, he has been so extraordinarily good and wise that, as a reward, he is permitted to choose his own form of Paradise. He chooses to return to earth and do good to man, and it is implied that he is possessed of powers, natural and supernatural, for the attainments of his ends to an almost unlimited extent.

As a theme, that is not new, but it has great possibilities. For instance, King Cole might have encountered a number of people, of all sorts and kinds, grateful and ungrateful, good, bad, weak, fanatical. In this case, the tale would turn on the stories of these characters, and the interest would be derived from the juxtaposition of man and man. This would be the romantic method. Or the poet might twist the theme into a tale of irony. King Cole, with his great gift and his innate simplicity, might find that in giving people their hearts' desires he did harm, not good. Such a rendering would find its importance in the obscure workings of atavism or environment. This would be the realistic method, so well employed in 'The Widow in the Bye Street.' Or again, the theme might concern itself with only one recipient of King Cole's favours, and make a picture of the gradual deterioration of the man gaining easily and more easily whatever he wishes, and the wishes growing more exorbitant and selfish as, one by one, they are gratified. That would be the psychological method. Again, King Cole might have been a subject of pure fantasy, a beautifully written fairy tale, relying more upon its treatment than its theme, making no pretense to either character-drawing, psychology, or irony, having no sub-structure, in fact, a story told for the sheer delight of the telling and the embroideries that can be wrought upon it. This would be the stylistic method.

Now any one of these methods would have been interesting. I do not say there are no others, but I cannot think of any of reasonable importance which may not be dropped into one of these four divisions. Mr. Masefield has found another method. It is none of these, but it does not justify itself and I am afraid it is really dull.

Mr. Masefield's 'King Cole' is not allegory, for nothing is worked out or even suggested; there is no reason why the circus people should be helped, and the helping is nothing more subtle than a bag of gold. It is not realism — and goodness knows the circus is a field for it — but this circus is as unconvincing as the cardboard figures in the toy theatres of our youth. It is not irony, because Mr. Masefield abhors the thing, except where his theme runs away with him and the facts of it are irony in the mere retailing, as in 'Dauber.' It is not psychology — 'The Knave of Hearts, he stole some tarts' better deserves the name. It is not style, for Mr. Masefield, a master of style when the mood is on him, was here writing solely to appease his dæmon, as is all too evident.

A travelling circus, sodden with rain and mud, discouraged, disgruntled, and worn, arrives at a town where they plan to give a show. But the town is harbouring royalty— the Prince and the Queen are come to lay a foundation stone (the only realistic touch in the book) — and the circus is forced to camp beyond the gates, where it is painfully likely that no one will come to see. King Cole, however, joins the party, consoles the showman with a platitudinous homily, and afterwards induces the royal pair, attended by the entire population of the town, to go to the performance. King Cole takes his place in the ring and, by playing on his flute, causes so magical a change in the performers that such a show was never seen before. A bag of gold is promptly given to the showman's wife by the amazed and delighted Prince, and the Queen orders a supper to be spread in a near-by tent for the actors. The crowning joy of this unique occasion is the arrival of the showman's long lost son in the character of sergeant in one of the regiments quartered in the town, longing to be reunited to his beloved parents. This edifying tale ends with the departure of the caravan for the next place in their itinerary and the vanishing of King Cole in a cloud of mist.

I do not say that this story could not have been carried by its style, if it had one. Unfortunately,

Mr. Masefield's style in this poem, whether in the large — the manipulation of design — or the small — the management of words, lines, and images — seems to have failed him. The poem is badly built and poorly presented.

There is one rule which holds good for all fiction, whether prose or poetry; it is that a scene must be laid in one of three places, it must be either here, there, or nowhere. 'Here' is now in time, and presupposes some place whose 'now' is synchronous with our own. In other words, 'here' may be in Iceland, Patagonia, Australia, or the Windward Islands, provided that the time be the present, and the characters act, dress, and speak as they should in those localities. American customs attributed to the Patagonians would dislocate the 'here.'

'There' refers to either time or place. It may be colonial America, Carthagena in the days of Hannibal, or eighteenth-century France. But wherever, in place or time, 'there' may be, no anachronisms should be tolerated. The drinking of afternoon tea in the White House, in Mr. Drinkwater's 'Lincoln,' is a literary blunder, for it violates the canon of the 'there.'

'Nowhere' is the vast land of the imagination, of fairy, what Barrie calls the 'Never Never Land.' It may also be the vision of disease or inebriety.

Descriptions of psychological states come under the head of 'nowhere,' as in certain kinds of fairy-stories, or ghost-stories, or a portrayal of delirium. These are plays within the play; the unity of the central theme is not broken. 'There' may also be interpolated into 'here,' as in dreams in which the dreamer steps backwards in time. In such cases, the central unity remains intact, there is no real confusion. But when anachronisms occur, when manners and customs of one place and time appear in another, the result is a shattered illusion, and to shatter an illusion is a severe fault in literary construction. Such faults come from either ignorance or carelessness, for every one who has studied the art of writing at all knows that this is the sort of thing which must not be done.

Mr. Masefield lays the scene of his poem in the 'here,' and with the arrival of King Cole it breaks quite legitimately into the 'nowhere.' The background of 'here' is static and untroubled, but superimposed upon it is 'nowhere,' an accepted convention which all readers perfectly understand. When Mr. Masefield begins to blur his 'here' with little dashes of 'there,' we can only imagine that he wrote in a hurry and did not sufficiently revise his manuscript. The scene is laid in England. When is not stated, and we are perfectly willing to believe it 'there' until we find a cowboy attached to the circus and the clowns smoking cigarettes; but suddenly we are introduced to a guard of knights and a procession of censer-bearing pages and we wonder, is this the fifteenth century? Then we come upon allusions to pouncet-boxes and cock-fighting, and courtiers 'wigged and starred' appear, so we think we have been mistaken, it is the eighteenth century; but that fades in the smoke of the clown's cigarettes, for cigarettes are indubitably of to-day. By this confusion, the real, which should have acted as a foil to the unreal, the 'nowhere,' is made shadowy and dim, and this in turn dims the 'nowhere,' and one effect of the poem is lost.

Mr. Masefield seldom employs the 'run-on' line in blank verse; his practice is almost as narrow as that of the eighteenth century in this respect. The flat-line manner is effective often, but it leads him to an awkward leaving out of the article before the noun in many cases and to such an obsolete construction as

Killing the clown his act for half his hire.

Mr. Masefield is addicted to the fishing-out of obsolete words, and frequently we thank him for resuscitating them; only when they are brought in purely for the rhyme, as in 'the drops glid' to rhyme with 'chid,' or 'legs besprad' to rhyme with 'had,' they are an annoyance.

It is another evidence of hasty writing for Mr. Masefield to let stand such a cacophonous couplet as

> Then came the crowd in-surging like the wave
> That closes up the gash the clipper clave.

But enough of the infelicities, for there are touches of Mr. Masefield's true genius here and there, in the description of the animals on page 17, and in the butterfly passage on page 52. How happy an expression, the 'sea-plunge of the evening star'! How pleasant the lines:

> Far overhead a rush of birds' wings sighed,
> From migrants going south until the spring.

Reading this book reminds one of Keats's advice to Shelley to 'load every rift with ore.' Dare we give the same advice to Mr. Masefield? At any rate, we may beg him to resist the wiles of publishers and not be hurried into unripe production.

A BIRD'S-EYE VIEW OF EDWIN
ARLINGTON ROBINSON

WHY does any one want a 'collected edition' of
anything? That is a question I often ask myself
when I turn from the shelves in my library where
the collected editions, each in the full panoply and
monotony of its uniform binding, stand in august
and unsympathetic splendour, to those other
shelves, crowded with faded and alluringly well-
read volumes, the first, or at least the early, un-
pretentious editions before the halo of 'collected'
was wrapped about the author's head. And yet,
even as I leave the half-calf, seventeen-volume
Browning for 'Paracelsus' in boards and 'Men and
Women' in faded green cloth, I know full well the
answer; for not all of us are sentimental book-
collectors or connoisseurs of literary vintages, and
even those of us who are, at times, these repre-
hensible things, may be, at other times, critics and
students, and to critics and students the 'collected
edition' is a handy tool. Yet, if a critic wish to
run his author to ground, he can by no means
ignore the earlier issues of his author's books. So
book-collectors are of some use other than the
sentimental, after all.

, Lazy readers like collected editions because, in buying them, they are sure of getting all of an author's books without the trouble of knowing their titles beforehand. Impecunious readers (by far the largest class everywhere at all times) get much for little, and this last is reason enough to account for the fondness of publishers for this particular article. Yet I can never help feeling that a 'collected edition' is something like a tombstone set at the head of its author's 'six feet of earth.' Of course, there is really nothing to prevent an author's adding new books to those already collected, nothing at all. But the very fact of their being a collection proclaims to the world not only that a man has done something, but that that something will, in all probability, be the major part of his production. If to call the 'collected' a tombstone already in place is going a bit far, we can at least consider that with it the 'six feet' are at any rate preëmpted, and the tombstone designed, with nothing lacking but the inscription.

Mr. Robinson's 'Collected Poems' does not intimidate by its voluminousness as Browning's seventeen volumes certainly do. But, as I heave its weight off the table beside me and strain my eyes over its narrow-spaced type, I sigh for the charming little volumes in which I am wont to read him; and, having collated the contents of this big book with the eight little ones, I put it down and read the poems for their poetry in the smaller volumes.

This 'Collected Poems' is valuable only for its cheapness, it costs less than the eight separate volumes put together, but there its value stops, unless we take it in some measure as accolade — an accolade by no means needed by the poet — and it is a little jarring to find a tombstone preparing for so very much alive and active a person as Mr. Robinson. Not only is he not written out, he is producing more rapidly every year. As to accolade, is it possible for any man to receive a greater tribute from his contemporaries than the spontaneous appreciations printed by the 'New York Times' on the occasion of his fiftieth birthday, two years ago?

Mr. Robinson has always been extremely reticent in, what I may call, *propria persona*. He writes poems for publication, never prose. He has given us no hint in any paper or review of his opinions of his fellow poets or himself, he has never put on record in ordinary speech his reactions to the literature of the past. He places no prefaces before his books; he and his poetry are indivisible; what we make of him is what we make of that, if we are the public. But it is just because of this that the collected edition becomes of real value to the student, for his exclusions and inclusions in the matter of poems do open up a certain insight into his mind. And what we chiefly make out is that Mr. Robinson started fully fledged and fully armed, that, to continue my extremely mixed metaphor, he has grown very few new feathers in the course of years, and that his sword has not only not been stropped since the beginning, it has not needed stropping.

There are various ways of collecting poems. The horrible way of the Browning editors has been to group together poems of a species, thus losing all the æsthetic value of the juxtaposition of a poem of one type with a poem of another type. Wise authors compose their books to obviate weariness. In a grouping by types, there is no escape for a reader but to close the book. Another way of collecting is the quasi-chronological, followed by Buxton-Forman in his Keats editions — the early poems come first and each book is given intact in the order of its first appearance. Still another way is the strictly chronological, in which separate books are entirely ignored and the poems are placed in the order in which they were written.

Mr. Robinson's plan has been none of these exactly, and, for a collection published in the poet's lifetime, the method he has adopted is excellent. He has kept his books intact throughout, but he begins with 'The Man Against the Sky' and follows it with his first volume, 'The Children of the Night.' After this, the books succeed one another in the sequence of their publication, except that 'Merlin' is interpolated between 'Captain Craig' and 'The Town Down the River,' for no reason that I can see unless to separate it from 'Lancelot.'

Here we are at once at a bit of personal criticism. For it is evident that Mr. Robinson agrees with the majority of his critics in considering 'The Man Against the Sky' his best book. He has made no changes in it, no changes in the order of the poems, that is. I have not sought for textual changes in many of the poems, but in those I have examined minutely there are none. In fact, the only volumes he has felt called upon to edit are 'The Children of the Night' and 'The Town Down the River,' and it is significant that he has dropped thirteen of the original poems from 'The Children of the Night' and only one from 'The Town Down the River.' A man who shows himself not averse to excisions on occasion, and yet who finds all he wishes to make (with one exception) in his earliest published work, proves his artistic career to have been singularly of a piece. This fact shows that if he and his creative faculty started together, his power of self-criticism has grown, for he has made no mistake in his excisions. The poems he has left out need cause no reader regret, except possibly the title poem of 'The Children of the Night,' and that is not so important as poetry as it is as revelation. Without it, the critic must begin with Mr. Robinson in mid-air.

Four years ago, I wrote an article on Mr. Robinson which was afterwards reprinted as the first chapter of my 'Tendencies in Modern American Poetry,' and nothing since has caused me to alter the opinions I there expressed. I have no space here to recapitulate the steps by which I reached my conclusions, but I can write nothing on Mr. Robinson without stating as a point of departure the main theme of my argument.

Let us begin at once by acknowledging that Mr. Robinson is the most finished and settled of the poets alive in America to-day. By 'finished' I mean accomplished, polished, master of his medium; by 'settled' I mean fixed and oriented in his own point of view and expression. If a contemporary dare to say that any living writer is sure to rank among the most important poets of his nation, I dare to say this of Mr. Robinson. Granting that, then, and admitting that contemporary judgment is a hazardous undertaking, let us see how and why he is what he is, and briefly consider that he is — what?

The main theme by which I set such store is that Mr. Robinson is a sort of temporal Colossus of Rhodes; he straddles a period. It seems to me almost impossible to understand Mr. Robinson without some knowledge of the society into which he was born. Recollect what Puritanism has meant to America, the good and the bad. Remember how long it held sway, and realize that this sway persisted much longer in the small towns and country districts than it did in the large cities. Mr. Robinson grew up in the seventies and eighties, and if any reader can recall from personal experience country New England in the seventies and eighties, no more need be said. This growing-up of Mr. Robinson's took place in Gardiner, a most charming little town on the Kennebec River in Maine. I love Gardiner myself, but I can imagine what it must have been like in the seventies and eighties. How Mr. Robinson could have started, as he did, in the heart of Gardiner, we cannot even conceive until we know more of him and his antecedents than we know now. From Gardiner he went to Harvard, and Harvard in the early nineties I do remember. Need I say that no one would have picked it for a forcing bed for Mr. Robinson's genius, but still it must have been an improvement on Gardiner.

Now Mr. Robinson is a dyed-in-the-wool New-

Englander, and that must never be forgotten.
His tenacity of purpose is thoroughly New England; so is his austerity and his horror of exuberance of expression. His insight into people is pure
Yankee shrewdness, as is also his violent and controlled passion. He is absolutely a native of his
place; the trouble was that he was not a native
of his time. He was twenty years ahead of his
time, and that advance has set the seal of melan-
choly upon him; or, to speak in the cant of the
day, it has wound him in inhibitions which he has
been unable to shake off.

This is why 'The Children of the Night' (the
poem, not the book) is so important. It shows Mr.
Robinson avowing a creedless religion. I say a
creedless religion advisedly, for I do not imagine
Mr. Robinson to be either an agnostic or an athe-
ist. But a creedless religion in Gardiner must have
made the holder of it feel as though branded with
the mark of Cain. Now evolution, in religion as in
other things, is a sane and salutary process which
leads to no bitterness and is merely the door to
freedom. Revolution, on the other hand, is the
bread of sorrow and the wine of despair. To be
called upon to do in oneself in a few years what
nations take centuries in bringing about, means a
severe wrenching of intellect and emotion. Read
Matthew Arnold's 'Dover Beach' and see what

the admitting of a creedless religion means to a
man brought up to a formal order, or, indeed, read
'The Children of the Night.' There is gain, of
course, but that is dim; there is loss, and that is
present and overwhelming.

Mr. Robinson could by no means be Gardiner,
he could by no means be America at that moment.
He began to see life with a touch of irony because
it was not his life. His life was nowhere, he withdrew mentally within himself; he withdrew more
and more, but he would not compromise. He
would be himself regardless of consequences, but
that self was an outsider. And, all the time, the
old order was holding him, shackling him; again
and again, he escaped, but it was one continuous
fight between himself and himself, between the old
Puritan atavism and the new, free spirit. Every
poem that Mr. Robinson writes is his dual self
personified. If he thought his own thoughts, he
could in no wise control the form in which he
set them; if he spoke his own direct speech, he
could put it to no unrestrained or novel music.
The luxuriance he innately feared, he drove away;
to him, it was an intellectual scarlet woman. He
cou'd not be happy, but he could be strong. He
could mutter 'Courage!' and nerve himself to
endurance. He looked to no future, he had no
time to build a new order and never guessed that

he was building it; he strove to keep himself, his point of view, above water, and he strove magnificently. This is what we read in 'The Children of the Night,' 'Captain Craig,' and 'The Town Down the River.' He raised for himself an altar, the success of failure, and at this he warmed his heart. It is a meagre flame, but it has sufficed him, and we must not quarrel that the pedestal is gaunt and severe.

Then, suddenly, in 1912, a new interest in poetry began to manifest itself. Mr. Robinson very likely did not think of himself as a part of it, at first; and I am sure that with much that has come to pass since he has been heartily out of sympathy. But, whatever he may have thought, he was its forerunner, he was even more than that, he was its oldest and most respected exemplar. And however the 'new poetry' may have affected Mr. Robinson, it brought his audience in its train. He had always been admired by a few; now that few widened to many. It is good for an artist to be admired, and 'The Man Against the Sky,' published six years after its predecessor, 'The Town Down the River,' shows a heightening of power in every direction. Before, he had written almost defiantly; now he is satisfied to write, now he has the contact of an audience to spur him on.

There is no new departure in 'The Man Against

the Sky' — Mr. Robinson struck his gait in 'The Children of the Night' and he has scarcely varied it since — but there is a greater ease and abundance. 'Flammonde' is one of the most beautiful poems in stanza form that Mr. Robinson has done, 'Ben Jonson Entertains a Man from Stratford' probably the best of his monologues; 'The Man Against the Sky' itself, an advance over 'The Children of the Night.' That poem was a cry; this is a question. The excellence of his early vignettes, 'John Evereldown,' 'Cliff Klingenhagen,' 'Richard Cory,' could hardly be surpassed, but there is a greater delicacy in 'Fragment,' a deeper tenderness in 'The Poor Relation,' an extraordinary weirdness and horror in 'Stafford's Cabin.' 'Captain Craig' contained 'Isaac and Archibald' and 'Aunt Imogen,' and nothing could be better in their kinds than these, but 'John Gorham' far outdoes 'The Woman and the Wife' and 'The Book of Annandale.'

Mr. Robinson is always at his best in contemporary scenes, and among contemporary people, with the brilliant exception of 'Ben Jonson.' His historical monologues are seldom apt as portraiture. 'An Island,' in which the dying Napoleon is the speaker, is false to its original in every line. Saint Paul addressing the Romans in 'The Three Taverns' is a daring attempt which utterly fails.

'Lazarus' lacks everything except its excellent execution. In 'Rahel to Varnhagen,' Mr. Robinson has been able to feel that his characters are contemporary, and to deal with them as though he had created them, and the result is a triumph of two people and an atmosphere.

Two people and an atmosphere is Mr. Robinson's forte. Crowd his stage as in 'Captain Craig,' or parts of 'Merlin' and 'Lancelot,' and his edge becomes blunted. It may be objected that 'Captain Craig' is virtually a monologue, but we can never forget the chorus of young men who are talked at, and the shadowy recorder who is occasionally permitted to speak. Mr. Robinson needs to feel his characters in intimate contact, which is very natural. Emotions run deeper and higher between two people who are in close relations with each other than they do in any other sort of grouping except that of a mob swayed by some over-mastering impulse. Mr. Robinson is too selective and secret to find inspiration in a mob. We cannot imagine his poems become the marching cry of a multitude. He builds his poetic world out of a series of poignant incidents, and by the deftest of little touches. The crumbling of Merlin's world is shown more vividly in the old man's appreciative dalliance with Vivian, than in his weary reception of the king's agonized ques-

tions. In 'Lancelot,' the hopeless fate of King
Arthur's realm does not lie for us on the battlefields strewn with dead knights, it is not in the
king's chamber at dawn, where Arthur, Gawaine,
and Bedivere await the first stroke of what all are
aware is doom, it is not even in the conversation
between Lancelot and the dying Gawaine; it is in
the meeting of Lancelot and Guinevere in the
garden, in their terrible interview by firelight
with the rain streaming over the deserted battlefields outside. It should be also in the final parting
of Lancelot and Guinevere in the convent parlour,
but it is not, for the single reason that the poem
is already spent emotionally before the end is
reached. This chill finale Mr. Robinson surely expected to be an epitome of the whole tragic tale,
but the parting of the lovers is too cool in its outward aspect to rouse his invention, and the final
scene is a succinct, but rather stereotyped, winding up.

In spite of Mr. Robinson's fine gift of irony, he
has a real liking for the melodramatic. Where the
human element is very powerful, this urge toward
melodrama is not too evident, it merely mutters
like a coming storm outside the scene on which the
event is staged; but where the human element is,
for any reason, weakened to the poet's mind,
melodrama runs foaming over the story. The

worst example of this is 'Avon's Harvest,' but there are many other cases in which the same thing happens in a greater or lesser degree: 'London Bridge,' for example, and 'The Valley of the Shadow,' and 'The Return of Morgan and Fingal.' There is not the slightest objection to melodrama as such, but when Mr. Robinson can skate the edge of it so successfully as he often does, to plunge in seems a lowering of technique. I believe that the reason for this sensation of lowering is because the poet's peculiar tenderness and pity are drowned out when mere event becomes too strenuous. For melodrama is circumstance due to external happening; tragedy is circumstance due to human emotion. A melodramatic occurrence such as Macbeth's murder of Banquo may rise to tragedy through its result upon human character. Shakespeare is forever using melodrama as the spark to light his tragedy, but with Mr. Robinson melodrama, when he indulges in it, is itself alone. Perhaps I should qualify this, as 'Stafford's Cabin,' 'Richard Cory,' and many other poems, skirt melodrama all the time by virtue of their subjects, but in these cases it is so obviously subordinate to the human scheme as scarcely to deserve its name.

I have spoken of Mr. Robinson's feeling for atmosphere. Never were pictures drawn with more economy than those he gives us, but they are

unforgettable. Since the first day I read it, I have
never forgotten how

> The cottage of old Archibald appeared.
> Little and white and high on a smooth round hill
> It stood, with hackmatacks and apple-trees
> Before it, and a big barn roof beyond;
> And over the place — trees, house, fields and all —
> Hovered an air of still simplicity
> And a fragrance of old summers.

Again, take the house in 'Fragment':

> Faint white pillars that seem to fade
> As you look from here are the first one sees
> Of his house where it hides and dies in a shade
> Of beeches and oaks and hickory trees.

'Merlin' is full of pictures, and they are no longer
of New England; we feel the difference at once, not
only in the scenes themselves, but in the more
elaborate wording with which they are presented:

> Gay birds
> Were singing high to greet him all along
> A broad and sanded woodland avenue
> That led him on forever, so he thought,
> Until at last there was an end of it;
> And at the end there was a gate of iron,
> Wrought heavily and invidiously barred.
> He pulled a cord that rang somewhere a bell
> Of many echoes, and sat down to rest,
> Outside the keeper's house, upon a bench
> Of carven stone that might for centuries
> Have waited there in silence to receive him.

The birds were singing still; leaves flashed and swung
Before him in the sunlight; a soft breeze
Made intermittent whisperings around him
Of love and fate and danger, and faint waves
Of many sweetly stinging fragile odors
Broke lightly as they touched him.

People are sketched quite as briefly and inevitably as places. Mr. Robinson has the gift of
epigrammatic expression. Flammonde comes from

> God knows where,
> With firm address and foreign air,
> With news of nations in his talk
> And something royal in his walk.

Richard Cory 'glittered when he walked.' Aaron
Stark's

> thin, pinched mouth was nothing but a mark;
> And when he spoke there came like sullen blows
> Through scattered fangs a few snarled words and close,
> As if a cur were chary of its bark.

Mr. Robinson is a master of brevity and exact,
straightforward speech in his poems, and that
makes his frequent habit of circumlocution appear
not a little odd and contradictory. It almost
seems as though Mr. Robinson were, at times,
afraid of his own theory of straightforward speech.
He refers to the characteristics of a certain gentleman as 'his index of adagios,' he speaks of billiard-
balls as 'three spheres of insidious ivory,' and calls

a hypodermic syringe 'a slight kind of engine.' I believe this sort of verbal juggling is an atavistic impulse — the same fear of the commonplace which produced the old poetical jargon which Mr. Robinson has done so much to banish from present-day poetry.

Allied to this tendency is the cryptic quality of much of his work. Although I do not believe for a moment that he realizes it, this cryptic quality is merely a poetic trick. All poets have their technical tricks, and all good poets make use of suggestion, but suggestion which has to be worked out like a puzzle, and half-statements confused in their own windings, are tricks carried a little too far. Browning was obscure because of a certain difficulty of expression; he triumphed in spite of it, not because of it. But Browning was crystal clear compared to Mr. Robinson in these cases. And Mr. Robinson has never the slightest difficulty in expressing himself. No, this is a poetic manner due to atavism, it is an evidence of the 'shackling' of which I have already spoken.

Edwin Arlington Robinson is a man of stark and sheer vision. He found his voice at a time when America was given over to pretty-prettinesses of all kinds. Some curious instinct for a harsher diet turned him to Crabbe. That alone would show how solitary a thing his development has been, for few poets have been more persistently neglected than George Crabbe. Mr. Robinson's sonnet on him begins by admitting the neglect:

> Give him the darkest inch your shelf allows,
> Hide him in lonely garrets, if you will, —
> But his hard, human pulse is throbbing still.

It is just the 'hard, human pulse' that Mr. Robinson craved for his own work. He is a far better poet than ever Crabbe was, because Crabbe saw only what is, while Mr. Robinson has a deep insight into why it is. In this, he is more akin to Thomas Hardy, whom he has celebrated in another poem in 'The Children of the Night,' omitted in this collected edition. In this poem, he speaks of himself as longing 'to feel once more a human atmosphere,' and this he finds in the 'grand sad song' which is Hardy's, given under the figure of a river. The poem ends:

> Across the music of its onward flow
> I saw the cottage lights of Wessex beam.

The hard, human pulse in Thomas Hardy is mellowed and deepened by a poetry of soul which Crabbe had not. Mr. Robinson has this poetry of soul to a far greater extent than Crabbe, but he has not yet attained to equality with Thomas Hardy. Hardy is no such poetical technician as Mr. Robinson, but he has a more probing understanding. Hardy touches his characters reverently, even as he dissects them; Mr. Robinson is not reverent, his nearest approach to it is a dry-eyed pity. Mr. Robinson has resisted life; Hardy has submitted to life as to a beloved master. Hardy is a great architect of tales and poems — 'The Dynasts' is monumental in conception and arrangement — but the details are inadequate; Mr. Robinson is a rare craftsman of detail, but his vision is pointillistic.

I have dwelt so long upon the juxtaposition of these two poets because such a juxtaposition makes clear what Mr. Robinson has and what he lacks. Thomas Hardy is a product of evolution, Mr. Robinson of revolution. His own lines in 'Lancelot' sum up his position not too badly:

> God, what a rain of ashes falls on him
> Who sees the new and cannot leave the old!

Mr. Robinson has left the old, but the dust of it on his shoes still impedes him at times, and he has struggled laboriously out of the rain of ashes although the white powder lingers on his coat.

Some critics have professed to find in Mr. Robinson's work the beating of the knell of doom. I think that is to mistake his attitude and the subtlety of his thought. Doom there may be, but it is an adjunct, not a preoccupation. His preoc-

cupation is with the unanswered question: Is the
Light real or imagined, is man dupe or prophet, is
faith unbolstered by logic an act of cowardice or
an expression of unconscious, pondering intel-
lectuality? There are poems of his to illustrate all
these angles of vision. He doubts himself into
cynicism, and rises from it through the conception
of unexplained beauty. He seeks below life for the
undercurrents by which he may discover its meaning. Sometimes he finds one thing, sometimes another; but, whatever he finds, the innate Puritan
fortitude and spirituality keep him to his quest.
He has not reached his goal nor found his Grail, but
he never turns aside from the search, continuing it
always with a wistful nobility of purpose which our
literature has not seen before.

The arrival of a belated admiration has had a
twofold effect upon the poet. It has induced a
more abundant creation, and it has urged his ambition to attempt things of larger scope. Here I
think we can say that Mr. Robinson has possibly
not been wise. The technique of the short or semi-
long poem, he has mastered completely; for the
long poem, he has been obliged to seek models.
'Merlin' as a series of intervals (particularly
lyric intervals) is excellent. As a whole long poem,
it is inchoate and without direction or climax.
These faults do not appear in 'Lancelot,' but

something else does. Mr. Robinson himself
abdicates in favour of many masters of the past.
The poem is built, not after a pattern, but to a
pattern. It is fine, moving, dramatic, but it is so
in just the manner hallowed by time. Mr. Robinson does manage to creep in here and there, but,
as a rule, some one else takes his place, not any
particular person — Mr. Robinson does not
plagiarise, but a fusion of dramatic poets all
speaking at once.

Mr. Robinson's old gospel of failure serves him
again in 'Lancelot.' The 'Light' he has always
believed in shines somberly across the poem, but,
more than in 'Merlin,' it seems a will-o'-the-wisp
gleam. The only hint of poignance in the end of
the poem is the very failure of the 'Light' to emit
any warm glow. Lancelot riding away, seeking to
comfort himself by this wan flame, is a pathetic
figure.

Mr. Robinson's poetry is pathetic, even when it
is most vigorous. There is infinite pathos in the
lot of the pioneer. Mr. Robinson is rather more an
outcast from an old order than an enthusiastic
adherent of a new. He is preoccupied with the
effort and pain of escape. Recognition has come
too late for him to experience the sharp joy which
lies in conscious upbuilding. It is almost as though
he regarded his achieved position with something